Data Strategy in Colleges and Universities

This valuable resource helps institutional leaders understand and implement a data strategy at their college or university that maximizes benefits to all creators and users of data. Exploring key considerations necessary for coordination of fragmented resources and the development of an effective, cohesive data strategy, this book brings together professionals from different higher education experiences and perspectives, including academic, administration, institutional research, information technology, and student affairs. Focusing on critical elements of data strategy and governance, each chapter in *Data Strategy in Colleges and Universities* helps higher education leaders address a frustrating problem with much-needed solutions for fostering a collaborative, data-driven strategy.

Kristina Powers is President of the Institute for Effectiveness in Higher Education.

Data Strategy in Colleges and Universities
From Understanding to Implementation

Edited by Kristina Powers

NEW YORK AND LONDON

First published 2020
by Routledge
52 Vanderbilt Avenue, New York, NY 10017

and by Routledge
2 Park Square, Milton Park, Abingdon, Oxon, OX14 4RN

Routledge is an imprint of the Taylor & Francis Group, an informa business

© 2020 Taylor & Francis

The right of Kristina Powers to be identified as the author of the editorial material, and of the authors for their individual chapters, has been asserted in accordance with sections 77 and 78 of the Copyright, Designs and Patents Act 1988.

All rights reserved. No part of this book may be reprinted or reproduced or utilised in any form or by any electronic, mechanical, or other means, now known or hereafter invented, including photocopying and recording, or in any information storage or retrieval system, without permission in writing from the publishers.

Trademark notice: Product or corporate names may be trademarks or registered trademarks, and are used only for identification and explanation without intent to infringe.

Library of Congress Cataloging-in-Publication Data
Names: Powers, Kristina, editor.
Title: Data strategy in colleges and universities : from understanding to implementation / edited by Kristina Powers.
Identifiers: LCCN 2019035206 | ISBN 9781138345973 (hardback) | ISBN 9781138345980 (paperback) | ISBN 9780429437564 (ebook)
Subjects: LCSH: Education, Higher–Data processing. | Universities and colleges–Planning.
Classification: LCC LB2395.7 .D37 2020 | DDC 378.0285–dc23
LC record available at https://lccn.loc.gov/2019035206

ISBN: 978-1-138-34597-3 (hbk)
ISBN: 978-1-138-34598-0 (pbk)
ISBN: 978-0-429-43756-4 (ebk)

Typeset in Perpetua
by Swales & Willis, Exeter, Devon, UK

Dedication

To my grandmother, Catherine—for nurturing my insatiable desire to learn and solve puzzles.

Contents

List of Figures ix
List of Tables x
Preface xi
Acknowledgments xv

PART I
Structure 1

1 The Value of Creating a Data Strategy 3
   KRISTINA POWERS AND STEVEN A. WEINER

2 Key Elements of a Data Strategy 14
   BRADEN J. HOSCH

3 Using Concepts from Strategic Planning 37
   ANGELA E. HENDERSON AND RESCHE D. HINES

4 Data Strategy versus Information Technology Planning 53
   SANDRA KINNEY AND JASON LEE WANG

PART II
Implementation 69

5 Leveraging Existing Information from Department Plans 71
   ERIN J. HOLMES

CONTENTS

6 Self-Appraisal of a Data Strategy — 84
LEAH EWING ROSS, JASON R. LEWIS, AND STEPHAN C. COOLEY

7 Anticipating Challenges and Offering Possible Solutions — 98
SHANNON ROSE LACOUNT AND MICHAEL J. WEISMAN

PART III
Perspectives — 115

8 Presidents' and Provosts' Perspectives — 117
IVAN L. HARRELL, II

9 Faculty Perspectives — 128
MICHAEL S. HARRIS, MOLLY K. ELLIS, AND KIM NELSON PRYOR

10 Student Affairs Leaders' Perspectives — 142
SHERI JONES

11 Institutional Researchers' Perspectives — 155
EREZ LENCHNER

12 Information Technology Analysts' Perspectives — 168
DEREK MACPHERSON

Biographies — 184
Index — 193

Figures

1.1	Disaggregated and Disconnected Data Strategy Model	8
1.2	Disaggregated and Aligned Data Strategy Model	9
1.3	Five Key Points for Securing Commitment	10
2.1	Key Elements of a Data Strategy	17
3.1	Foundational Planning Components	39
3.2	Summary of Planning Processes	40
3.3	Key Questions for Consideration	47
3.4	DATA Analysis	50
4.1	Data Strategy Environment	54
4.2	Information Technology Planning Cycle	60
4.3	Data Planning and Management Strategy Framework	67
5.1	Two Models of Institutional Research	71
5.2	Data–Information–Knowledge–Wisdom Model	73
6.1	Self-Appraisal of a Data Strategy: Overview of the How	88
6.2	Self-Appraisal of a Data Strategy: Details of the How	88
7.1	Eight Challenges and Solutions	99
7.2	Scenario 1	104
7.3	Scenario 2	106
7.4	Scenario 3	107
8.1	Difficult Components of the President and Provost Positions	118
8.2	Key Points that Presidents and Provosts Want Data Experts to Understand	123
10.1	Data Strategy Questions for Consideration When Proposing Initiatives	148
10.2	Current Challenges in Getting and Using Data	149
10.3	Methods-Focused vs Action-Focused Agendas	153
11.1	The Role of IR Professionals in a Data Strategy	160
12.1	Generic Example of a Data Warehouse Supporting an Academic Institution	169

Tables

2.1	Key Elements of a Data Strategy	17
2.2	Examples of Analytics Outputs	31
3.1	Summary Comparison of Strategic Planning and Data Strategy Elements	47
4.1	Comparison of Data Strategy and IT Plan	61
9.1	Sub-Types of Non-Tenure-Track Faculty	129
9.2	Examples of Formative and Summative Assessments	133
12.1	Frequent IT Data Positions	172
12.2	Terms Commonly Used by IT Analysts	175

Preface

In an era of big data, there seems to be more data, yet fewer answers, in all industries and sectors. No group of organizations has really figured out how to make the most effective and efficient use of data—yet. Additionally, employees across the board, from analysts to senior leaders, are dissatisfied with their current data access, the wait time for results, and the complexity of completing ostensibly simple reports, to name but a few areas in need of improvement.

To this dissatisfaction with current data conditions we bring an optimism that it is possible to leverage improved tactics and new technology. To put it bluntly, there has to be a better way to manage this data chaos. While there are plenty of books and articles devoted to either data *or* strategy, this is the first to address the two combined—data strategy—in the context of higher education. Any group that is the first to publicly share their thoughts, ideas, and research on a topic takes pride in advancing new knowledge but acknowledges that their efforts are only the beginning and that much work remains to be done. This is true of the 20 authors across 13 colleges, universities, and organizations who contributed to this book.

AUTHORS' AIM AND BOOK ORGANIZATION

The authors aim to help institutional leaders understand and implement a data strategy at their college or university, to maximize benefits to all data users and creators. Exploring key considerations in the development of an effective data strategy, this book brings together professionals with different higher education experiences and perspectives, including faculty, administrators, and experts in institutional research, information technology (IT), and student affairs. Each chapter focuses on critical elements of a data strategy and concludes with key discussion questions that can be used in graduate courses, around the conference table, or with boards of trustees.

PREFACE

The book is broken down into three parts:

Part I: Structure—Since having a data strategy is not yet commonplace in colleges and universities, the first four chapters (Part I) contextualize and explain the topic. These chapters are purposefully designed to build on readers' existing knowledge about strategic planning and data use to educate them about data strategy. Chapter 1 focuses on why colleges and universities should care about creating a data strategy and the advantages of having one. Chapter 2 discusses the components of a data strategy so that institutions can utilize one or more common models when creating their own.

Chapter 3 explores strategic planning as it relates to data strategy and helps readers connect familiar strategic planning topics to an unfamiliar data strategy. Institutions may already have an IT plan and wonder if a data strategy is the same thing. Chapter 4 discusses the drastic differences between a data strategy and an IT plan—and advocates that both are crucial.

Part II: Implementation—While some individuals have a good vision for change, effectively implementing ideas may be more difficult. The three chapters in Part II give readers clear steps and tactics for implementing a data strategy. Chapter 5 explains how to leverage existing information so that colleges and universities can use what they already have first. Certain departments may have data strategy elements in their existing departmental plans.

Since an honest self-appraisal of current institutional planning efforts can yield both key insights into pain points and possible solutions, Chapter 6 provides detailed steps for performing this process. Creating a data strategy will be challenging for most institutions because they have not completed the process before. Recognizing this fact, Chapter 7 addresses the issues that may be preventing the institution from naturally moving forward.

Part III: Perspectives—A person's perspective is their reality. Since understanding different versions of reality can be useful in creating and advancing a data strategy, Part III explores the perspectives of five different groups of data users and providers and the different challenges they face. Chapter 8 focuses on presidents and provosts, who have enormous responsibilities and need accurate and timely data to meet internal decision making and external audience demands. Chapter 9 looks at faculty, who both create data and constantly use disparate qualitative and quantitative information to assess student learning and improve academic programs.

Students are the largest group of decision makers at a college or university. Providing them with tools and information to make informed decisions is critical and does not happen by accident. Supporting student success requires both a thorough understanding of the particular student population involved and the simultaneous collaboration of multiple departments. Chapter 10 addresses the challenges student affairs leaders must navigate as consumers of data.

Chapter 11 is devoted to institutional researchers, who are typically responsible for providing data to internal and external stakeholders. Finally, Chapter 12 turns to IT analysts, who often play a critical role in collecting the data and in some cases extracting the data from data systems for use by decision makers.

Added Value to the Field of Higher Education

The 20 authors who contributed to this book are passionate about higher education (as you will see when reading their biographies). We are all committed to strengthening colleges and universities and, even more importantly, student success. It is these shared interests and values that have brought us together to create this book, which has the following benefits:

- It meets a growing and unmet need for guidance on effectively managing data resources so that the all data users and providers are collectively working toward the same institutional goals rather than taking separate, fragmented approaches.
- It is the first book in the higher education sector to focus on creating a data strategy.
- Its chapters are written from different perspectives of leaders within higher education, making it relevant to a large segment of readers.
- Many business-related books in this field target chief information officers with IT strategies for using big data. This book goes beyond the role of the CIO and big data, weaving together fragmented, department-level data strategies into a cohesive institutional data strategy.
- Each chapter includes discussion questions that can be used by faculty in graduate courses or by senior leaders (executives, boards of trustees, committees, etc.) for planning.

COMPANION BOOK ON DATA CULTURE

It is nearly impossible to discuss data strategy without discussing data culture. While data culture is at least alluded to in every chapter, it is not the focus of this book. Data culture is a large enough topic to deserve its own separate book—and one exists. Those who are serious about creating a data strategy for their institution may wish to consult *Cultivating a Data Culture in Higher Education* (edited by K. Powers and A. Henderson, 2018).

xiii

PREFACE

Since most institutions have already established a data culture, *Cultivating a Data Culture in Higher Education* focuses on improvement. With the rapidly expanded use of data across institutions, different data cultures have developed organically—some positive, others less so. Senior leaders have recognized this discourse and need to shape the culture. *Cultivating a Data Culture in Higher Education* identifies ways in which institutions can foster a collaborative, forward-moving data-driven environment centered on people.

Very few colleges or universities have created an institutional data strategy. Leaders thus have an exciting opportunity to shape this undertaking without having to contend with historical precedents or previous experiences. *Data Strategy in Colleges and Universities* focuses on the *work* of data creators and requests by data users to promote a planned and purposeful effort that is directly tied to strategic goals. This book helps leaders tackle many frustrating problems with a single solution: the creation of a data strategy.

ENJOY AND SHARE

We hope that you enjoy the book and that it will be of use to you in developing a data strategy at your institution. Readers are invited to reach out and share their experiences of creating a data strategy. This information will be used to highlight successes and address challenges in future publications and presentations. You can email me at KP@InstituteforEffectiveness.org or visit the Institute for Effectiveness in Higher Education at www.InstituteforEffectiveness.org

Acknowledgments

I would like to express heartfelt appreciation to those who have made this book possible. First, I would like to acknowledge all of the chapter authors who contributed their time and expertise. It is with great gratitude that I thank Routledge, especially my editor—Heather Jarrow and her team, with whom I have now worked on four books. I am privileged to work with the dedicated and experienced team at Routledge.

I would like to thank the anonymous individuals who took the time to respond to Routledge's survey questionnaire which guided the development of the book. I have incorporated much of the feedback and comments that consistently emerged; your early contributions resulted in an enhanced and robust publication.

I deeply admire the editing expertise of Tracy Kendrick. Her attention to detail combined with passion for her profession, was the patina on this collective effort. I am thrilled that Tracy was willing to apply her exceptional editing skills to this book.

Finally, an honorable mention goes to the family and friends of all contributors to this book; it is with their support that we are able to complete the research about which we are so passionate.

Part I
Structure

Chapter 1

The Value of Creating a Data Strategy

Kristina Powers and Steven A. Weiner

INTRODUCTION

What is a data strategy anyway? And why would anyone want one? Colleges and universities already invest significantly in both data (dedicated staff, information technology systems, etc.) and strategy (planning, budgeting, etc.). Isn't there enough emphasis on data and strategy? What more can be done in this space? There are plenty of books and articles devoted to either data or strategy, but oddly enough, this is the first to address the two combined—data strategy—in the context of higher education.

This chapter focuses on why institutions should care about creating a data strategy and the gains achieved by having one. In particular, we begin by describing what a data strategy is and why institutions should have one. We then outline the characteristics of a data strategy. Examining the benefits of a data strategy and the risks of not having one is vital to securing buy-in from senior leaders. Thus, we conclude the chapter with five key steps to securing commitment to an institution-wide data strategy. While these steps are geared towards senior leaders, they can be used with key stakeholder groups as well.

THE PROBLEM: MORE DATA, FEWER ANSWERS

Leaders across organizations—including institutions of higher education—concur that data are critical to management and decision-making. Over the past two decades, data has expanded into every corner of colleges and universities. At this point, it is difficult to find a department that has not become more data-driven.

As the number of data creators and users has increased, so too has the variety of approaches to providing leaders with data and analyses. In more than a few instances, that dynamic has created conflicting information. Such inconsistencies can frustrate senior leaders, who are ultimately responsible for the success (or failure) of their institution. They are left wondering which numbers are the "right" ones and how to sift through the volumes of reports to know which numbers really matter.

In an era of "big data," why does it feel as if there is an inverse relationship between volume and quality of data? Many leaders have been patiently awaiting the fulfillment of promises of improved tools for data-driven decision making. However, in most cases, technology "enhancements" have led to what seem to be fewer answers and increased wait times for pressing inquiries.

One of the root problems is that many data analysts spend only 20% of their time actually analyzing data (the rest is spent on data preparation). This issue is only going to get worse without change (Aiken & Harbour, 2017). Perhaps because of the increased availability of data and the improved tools for analyzing it, ensuring the integrity and effective use of data are becoming more and more of a challenge for colleges and universities.

It is a reasonable expectation that senior leaders should be able to ask both simple and complex questions and get comprehensive answers in a realistic timeframe. After all, smart, capable, qualified, experienced professionals have been employed to do this work. This prompts the question: What is the magic formula that allows data creators to work together, avoid duplication, and focus on strategic priorities? This seems like a tall task—and it is—without a *data strategy for colleges and universities*.

WHAT IS A DATA STRATEGY?

While most people in higher education are familiar with terms such as "strategic planning" and "data analysis," the term "data strategy" may be new to many. However, it is not new to those in industries outside of higher education. Here is a simple and straightforward definition: "A plan to help set direction relative to data and how the organization will use it in direct support of their organizational strategy" (Aiken & Harbour, 2017, p. 14).

Lahanas's (2014) definition of what a data strategy is *not* may enhance the discussion:

- A data strategy is not a list of generic principles or obvious statements (such as "data are an enterprise asset").
- A data strategy is not merely a laundry list of technology trends that might somehow influence the organization in coming years.
- A data strategy is not a vague list of objectives without a clear guiding vision or path for actualization.

- A data strategy is not merely the top-level vision either, it can expand into critical data domains such as "business intelligence" and eventually represent a family of strategies.

(Lahanas, 2014, p. 1)

The responsibility for establishing a data strategy should not fall to an individual department. Rather, the impetus must occur at the institutional level, much like other strategic efforts, such as planning, budgeting, building, and capital campaigns; Chapter 2 elaborates on this with a deep dive into the key elements of a data strategy.

THE VALUE OF CREATING A DATA STRATEGY

Creating a data strategy requires a coordinated effort that efficiently and effectively marshals resources in pursuit of institutional goals rather than the needs of individual departments or units. Attempts to achieve the same results by establishing "one source of the truth" have failed because these systems stifle the very thing desired: use of data by many. More contemporary solutions leverage collaboration and organizational strategies to manage a complex problem.

For example, typically when there is a valued resource, such as money, it is managed at the highest level, in this case by the chief financial officer. It would be counterproductive for each department to develop its own budget policies and procedures independently. Yet institutions frequently have multiple approaches to collecting, producing, and analyzing data.

An institutional data strategy integrates data collection and analysis elements from throughout the entire organization into one unified plan and set of goals. Similar to an institutional strategic plan, a data strategy allows different units the flexibility to develop their own data and analysis goals while aligning with those of the institution. This approach respects the individuality of departments while minimizing the haphazardness of having multiple systems and processes.

Goals are not attained by accident. Coordination of resources, both human and financial, increases the chances of success. Institutions invest in strategy because it is too costly not to efficiently coordinate resources pivotal to achieving goals. Data resources merit the same level of attention given to people and money.

BENEFITS OF A (GOOD!) DATA STRATEGY

"A good data strategy is not determined by what data is readily or potentially available—it's about what your business wants to achieve, and how data can help you get there" (Marr, 2017, p. 21). Organizations have invested heavily in data efforts over the last decade to enable data-driven decision making that maximizes the efficient and effective use of resources. Key among those investments are personnel and infrastructure (such as data warehouses).

In a multi-decade era of "doing less with more," using data to meet unfunded mandates was a logical approach. And it worked. Institutions are making more decisions based on data. Now they need to adopt a data strategy to ensure that the right data are produced at the right time and in the right way.

The U.S. Department of Defense's Chief Data Officer noted that "Direction is more important than speed. If you're pointed in the wrong direction, it doesn't matter how fast you're traveling. Inversely, if you're locked on to your desired destination, all progress is positive, no matter how slow you're going" (Conlin, 2019, p. 1). We can't emphasize this enough: it is important to create a good data strategy, not just any data strategy.

Collect Only Useful Data

Adelman, Moss, and Abai (2005) found that "most major corporations and large government organizations have three-to four-fold needless data redundancy—data that exists for no other reason than failure to properly plan and implement" (p. xxiii). The value of routine reporting is too seldom questioned, consuming personnel time that could be better spent on more high-value efforts that produce information on which decisions can be based. Data needs evolve over time, whether due to changes in leadership or changes in the world around us—or both. And yet, all too frequently, routine data reporting keeps flowing, leading to reports that no one reads and thus no one acts upon.

"Having a clear data strategy is also critical when you consider the sheer volume of data that is available these days" (Marr, 2017, p. 17). The sheer volume of data reporting can overwhelm managers. An effective data strategy will periodically analyze whether more streamlined or otherwise refocused data reporting would lead to more and better actionable information for decision makers.

Misguided data collection and reporting is also a factor with ad hoc efforts, such as the use of surveys within a college or university. A group wishing to send out a survey on a particular topic (student experience, satisfaction with a service, ideas for new programs or services, etc.) will draft a series of questions. More often than not, at least a few of these questions will produce data of uncertain value. Survey designers do not always ask, "How will I use the information I am going to collect?" Some are driven to ask questions just because they can! Equally misguided is the rationale: "We thought it would be nice to know" or "we are collecting it just in case." In case of what?

THE VALUE OF CREATING A DATA STRATEGY

With electronic surveys, people can fall into the illusion that data collecting is free—so why not collect everything? However, burdensome surveys reduce response rates. Analyzing, storing, and reporting data have costs that are not justifiable if the data are not used. And managers in receipt of survey reports that include data elements of uncertain value may discredit other aspects of the survey results. One of the benefits of a data strategy is that it pushes the institution to seriously discuss and create collection criteria so that all data gathered has value—and is used. Moreover, leadership must have the discipline to ensure that such discussions take place at regular intervals.

Leverage Expanded Data Literacy

As the ability to access data using technology has expanded, so too has data literacy among employees. Over the last few decades, it has become common to find data-literate people sprinkled throughout an institution rather than being housed in one or two offices. While it is good news that more people have these skill sets, ability levels vary widely.

An unintended consequence of this distributed data model is that multiple people can and do work on the same request without others knowing. Worse yet, they often arrive at different results (which frustrates presidents considerably; see Chapter 8). Having a data strategy in place ensures that all data makers and users (essentially the entire college or university) work in an integrated manner that aligns with the institution's mission and strategic planning goals.

Bring Data Creators Together

A data strategy melds data analysis efforts from multiple departments into a cohesive plan; otherwise, "The absence of a data strategy gives a blank check to those who want to pursue their own agendas" (Adelman, Moss, & Abai, 2005, p. 3). Most colleges and universities currently have a disaggregated set of departments using data, with perhaps a few working together from time to time, as shown in Figure 1.1. Overall, they each have their own independent and unaligned data strategy—whether written or not.

In Figure 1.2, departments or functions maintain their independence, but their data strategies are all aligned to the institution's rather than fragmented. We are not suggesting that all data creators and users need to report to one vice president. If that works for your institution, great. However, there are precedents for not having all similarly focused staff report to one vice president. For example, all employees who spend institutional dollars do not report to the chief financial officer, and institutions still find ways to develop

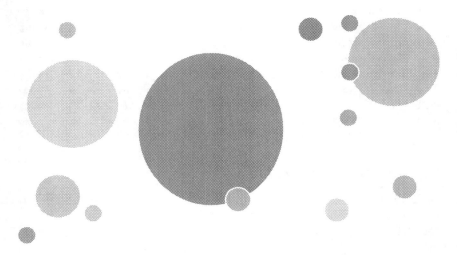

FIGURE 1.1 Disaggregated and Disconnected Data Strategy Model

and implement a budget. The same is true of people who use computers and information technology.

ONBOARDING SENIOR LEADERS TO COMMIT TO THE EFFORTS

Getting senior leaders interested in creating a data strategy is the easy part. Who wouldn't support an organized effort to maximize one of their institution's most important and valuable assets—data? Leaders are frustrated by the length of time it takes to obtain data to answer simple questions, as well as by inconsistencies in the analysis of (what should be) the same data elements. Jaded leaders could assume that an institution-wide solution whereby all departments with access to data use that data efficiently and effectively is too good to be true.

Leaders should be encouraged to think holistically about data needs. Which areas are essential to steering an organization, and which data best indicates how well those areas are performing? Senior staff need to have confidence in the integrity of their data sources in order to be assured of quality reporting. To get there, leaders need to be invested in effective processes, appropriate controls, solid technology, and clear roles and responsibilities throughout the data lifecycle within their organization. Only then can they enjoy the peace of mind of knowing that the reports they receive are actionable. Today's colleges and universities have invested heavily in information

THE VALUE OF CREATING A DATA STRATEGY

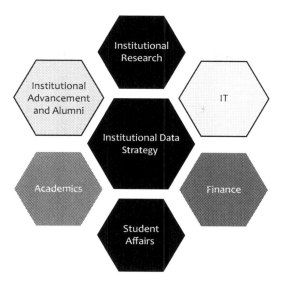

FIGURE 1.2 Disaggregated and Aligned Data Strategy Model

resources and must leverage that investment effectively to realize its full potential.

Leaders should also be made to consider the considerable cost they incur in the absence of a data strategy.

> On average, less than 50% of structured data is used in making decisions—and less than 1% of an organization's unstructured data is analyzed or used at all. More than 70% of employees have access to data they should not, and 80% of analysts' time is spent simply discovering and preparing data.
> (Davenport, 2017, p. 1)

The remainder of this chapter focuses on five key points for securing commitment to an institution-wide data strategy (Figure 1.3).

Use Discipline and Persistence to Meet Goals

Like a strategic plan, a successful data strategy requires work, coordination, and a commitment from leadership and other key generators and users of data throughout a college or university. Just as it takes discipline and persistence to create an annual budget or strategic plan, so too will discipline and persistence be essential to the development of an effective data strategy. And just like budgeting and planning, data strategy is not a once-and-done phenomenon.

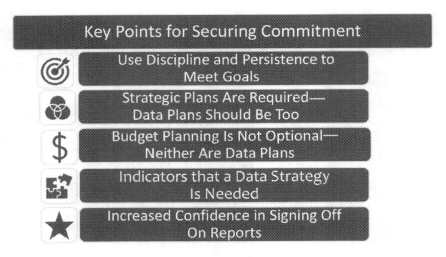

FIGURE 1.3 Five Key Points for Securing Commitment

Imagine if leadership said that creating an annual institutional budget was optional this year. How many institutions would actually create a budget? Because there is a commitment by leadership to spend financial resources efficiently and effectively—and most importantly, not overspend—leadership holds all budget managers to account. The same level of tenacity and accountability must accompany a data strategy.

Strategic Plans Are Required—Data Plans Should Be Too

As a leader, you may think, "Well, this and many other institutions have been successful without a data strategy. Is a plan really necessary?" Consider that strategic planning began in the 1960s and by the 1980s was commonplace. We now take for granted that strategic plans are essential for community buy-in, board oversight, and effective communication of institutional goals. We now accept as fact that a well-conceived strategic plan is vital to ensuring that all departments of an institution are working towards the same goals.

We also now take for granted that it is much easier and more productive to go through the strategic planning process of discussion, discourse, and debate so that ideas and comments are heard before final goals and priorities are determined. While every college or university employee may not align all aspects of their day-to-day work with a strategic plan, many will cite it as a basis for prioritizing their efforts, as well as for its utility in developing a sense of common purpose.

THE VALUE OF CREATING A DATA STRATEGY

Employees tend to use strategic plans as a guiding force for their work. Just as business investors insist on seeing and critiquing a strategic plan before they will consider making a financial commitment, so too do many vital constituencies of a college or university. Chapter 3, Using Concepts from Strategic Planning by Henderson and Hines, delves into ways that the existing strategic planning process can be leveraged to create a data strategy.

Budget Planning Is Not Optional—Neither Are Data Plans

When asking yourself if a data strategy is really necessary, consider how effectively the institution could be managed without a budget, which is, in effect, a financial plan. If, as a leader, you manage other important resources (money and people) through the use of a plan, why wouldn't data—a critical resource for the effective oversight of a college or university—merit the same level of attention?

> Without a smart plan of action to use the data to produce business insights, the data itself becomes a white elephant—expensive and useless. Therefore, if companies want to avoid drowning in data, they need to develop a smart strategy that focuses on the data they really need to achieve their goals. In other words, this means defining the business-critical questions that need answering and then collecting and analyzing only that data which will answer those questions.
>
> (Marr, 2017, p. 17)

Indicators that a Data Strategy Is Needed

As a senior leader, it is reasonable to ask, "How do I know whether my institution needs a data strategy?" Adelman, Moss, and Abai (2005) identify issues that signal a need for a data strategy. We selected the following relevant items and expanded on each within the higher education context:

- Dirty data
- Redundant data
- Inconsistent data
- Inability to integrate data
- Poor availability of data
- Data users who are dissatisfied with availability and timeliness of analyses
- Feeling that there are a lot of data leaders but no one bringing the data together.

Increased Confidence in Signing Off on Reports

Senior-level sign off is frequently required before data can be submitted (to auditors, donors, government agencies, accrediting bodies, annual report recipients, athletic association partners, etc.). All too often, those same senior leaders have little confidence in the accuracy of the data. Leaders would feel more confident attesting to the accuracy of the data if reports were produced within the context of a sound data strategy (Adelman, Moss, & Abai, 2005). A sound data strategy should be synonymous with reliable data sources and effective data governance. With the right controls, technology, and oversight, data confidence rises.

And confidence in data quality is essential. Leaders who are confident about the underlying data are able to rely upon it to identify both problems and opportunities, make decisions, and manage risks. When leaders have that confidence, they can not only sign off on reports but also address the needs of their institution more effectively.

> **DISCUSSION QUESTIONS**
>
> 1. This chapter provided a definition of a data strategy as well as examples of what a data strategy is not. What two to three additional examples can you add to the list of "what a data strategy is not" that would be relevant for your institution type and culture?
> 2. Five strategies for getting senior leaders to commit to creating a data strategy were discussed. Which two strategies would you use with your supervisor? With your senior leaders? What responses do you anticipate, and how would you reply to them?
> 3. Consider three departments at your institution that use or create data/information. In what ways would they benefit from a shared data strategy? How would the institution benefit from those departments having a data strategy?
> 4. Connecting the data strategy to the institutional mission and strategic plan is key to keeping all stakeholders focused and aligned. What aspects of the mission and strategic plan would you emphasize when creating a data strategy at your institution?
> 5. Describe the steps you might take to engage senior leaders as well as key stakeholder groups in discussing development of a data strategy.

REFERENCES

Adelman, S., Moss, L., & Abai, M. (2005). *Data strategy*. Addison-Wesley: Upper Saddle River, NJ.

Aiken, P., & Harbour, T. (2017). *Data strategy and the enterprise data executive: Ensuring that business and IT are in synch in the post-big data era*. Technics Publications. Kindle Edition.

Conlin, M. (2019). Data science 101: A CDO's viewpoint. LinkedIn Post. Retrieved from https://media.licdn.com/dms/document/C4D1FAQGdsdh6GdhA2A/feedshare-document-pdf-analyzed/0?e=1557320400&v=beta&t=6_18G0RILmAldm5v_mQDobED287R4tOdvIv1-n_Tirc

Davenport, T. (2017). What's your data strategy? *Harvard Business Review*. Retrieved from https://hbr.org/webinar/2017/04/whats-your-data-strategy

Lahanas, S. (2014). Why organizations need a data strategy. *Dataconomy*. Retrieved May 30, 2018 from http://dataconomy.com/2014/11/why-organizations-need-a-data-strategy

Marr, B. (2017). *Data strategy: How to profit from a world of big data, analytics and the internet of things*. Kogan Page. Kindle Edition.

Chapter 2

Key Elements of a Data Strategy

Braden J. Hosch

INTRODUCTION

As discussed in Chapter 1, a data strategy is an intentional action plan to capture, integrate, and use data to advance an institution's mission and goals. This chapter seeks to extend beyond theory into practice by describing seven key elements of an effective data strategy: (1) data acquisition; (2) data governance; (3) data quality; (4) data access; (5) data literacy and usage; (6) data extraction and reporting; and (7) data analytics. Many of these can be reconfigured to fit organizational context and maturity, but all must remain present in some form. By incorporating these components in its data strategy, an institution will ensure the availability of sufficient quality data to advance the institution's mission and goals.

The maturity and sophistication of each of these elements are context-specific as well as specific to each major data store or system housing data of value, more broadly termed "data assets." While a fully realized institutional data strategy ultimately encompasses all data created or used by the institution, in practice the development of a data strategy and the articulation of its key elements require scope-based prioritization. For instance, a college will likely place high priority on its enterprise system for students and faculty, such as Banner or PeopleSoft, and integration with course-evaluation platforms and learning-management systems, but might delay full integration with systems for advancement and faculty research data to later phases.

Such decisions should be informed by institutional priorities and goals as well as a return on investment analysis. One consideration, for example, would be the extent to which integrating student-information systems (course grades, addresses, etc.) with faculty research data stores (data sets for NSF research, archival documents for historical monographs) would produce value for the institution and advance its goals. Since little value would likely be added, faculty research data stores might be placed outside the scope of initial phases of the data strategy.

DATA VISION

Much like a vision statement is a forward-looking articulation of what an organization would like to become, a data vision statement indicates how data will help an organization realize its mission and strategic goals. Importantly, the data vision should not focus on IT but rather highlight how data can benefit people and operations (a point further emphasized in Chapter 4 – Data Strategy Versus and Information Technology Planning). The British Library (2017), for instance, has formulated this strong and straightforward statement: "Our vision for the British Library is that research data are as integrated into our collections, research and services as text is today" (p. 1).

Colleges and universities should consider how such a statement supports their context, mission, goals, and resources. An aggressive approach might be to advocate integrating the university's data assets in the same way that devices are networked today. Articulating a vision of this scope would highlight the need to deploy significant resources for its realization, much like IT has invested in networking staff, infrastructure, policies, and risk management.

Alternatively, the vision might be less resource intensive but still forward-looking. For instance, the statement might emphasize how people interact with data: students, faculty, and staff will use data assets the way that they use email today. The difference in focus between these two examples illustrates the importance of deliberating about an organization's data vision; the future it articulates will drive decision making, resource allocation, and prioritization. A clear statement of data vision will guide how an institution approaches the subsequent components of its data strategy.

KEY ELEMENTS OF A DATA STRATEGY

Even though the concept of an organizational data strategy is a relatively new development in industry and only nascent in higher education, some models have been advanced to articulate the basic components and approaches. Levy (2018) breaks down an organizational data strategy into five core actions in an organizational data strategy: (1) identification of data and its meaning; (2) storage of data in persistent structures; (3) provisioning of data to make it reusable; (4) processing of data to combine data residing in disparate systems; and (5) governance of data to promote effective usage.

In another approach, Carruthers and Jackson (2018) suggest that new chief data officers develop an immediate data strategy encompassing six components: (1) stability and rationalization; (2) data culture and governance; (3) existing IT initiatives; (4) data exploitation and integration; (5) data performance and quality; and (6) data security. The target data strategy described subsequently is more of a guide for organizational change management than an action plan.

While these approaches offer some useful guidance, they generally do not provide sufficient detail about what needs to be considered and done to craft and implement a data strategy in the context of higher education. This chapter elaborates on a data strategy framework developed by Stony Brook University, an internationally ranked research institution (Hosch, 2017). The seven components, shown in Table 2.1, are described in greater detail herein, offering more direction for how to develop and launch a data strategy at any college or university. Notably, these components may differ among data assets depending on their priority and relationship to institutional goals and operational needs.

DATA ACQUISITION

Simply put, data acquisition is how an institution of higher education obtains its data. Employees and students generate data internally, and data also comes from outside sources. Colleges and universities already acquire data through the admissions process, teaching and learning, and administrative operations, of course, but the process for doing so has in general been reactive and unsystematic. For instance, the admissions office at the request of leadership may conduct a competitive analysis and so obtain data from the National Student Clearinghouse (NSC) about where non-enrolling applicants eventually matriculated, but NSC data may not be stored or regularly reused. The financial aid office receives reports from the federal government about the repayment status of former students who borrowed educational loans, but the data may be stored in Excel files on a desktop computer. The advancement office may maintain all of its records in a separate system for donor management. In all of these instances, the institution has acquired data, but absent a formal data strategy, these data assets will not be leveraged to their fullest extent. An effective data acquisition strategy involves six activities.

Activity 1: Identification

An early step in formulating a data strategy is to establish and maintain an inventory of data assets and assess the maturity of acquisition processes. Kiron (2017) documents the importance of a deliberately constructed and managed data inventory. This inventory may be large and will grow. Data in the

KEY ELEMENTS OF A DATA STRATEGY

Table 2.1 Key Elements of a Data Strategy

Data Acquisition	Data Governance
How the institution obtains its data. Build an inventory of data assets. For each one, establish a written plan for: - Identification - Prioritization - Capture - Storage - Linkage - Curation	How people make decisions and behave with respect to how data will be defined, produced, used, stored, and destroyed. Establish: - Decision making body and rules - Data dictionaries - Data stewards

Data Quality	Data Access
How data will be maintained to be complete, valid, consistent, timely, and accurate to make them appropriate for a specific use.	How authorized individuals can obtain and use data while maintaining privacy and security. Establish written plans for: - Accessibility - Security

Data Usage & Literacy	Data Extraction & Reporting	Data Analytics
How data users understand and use data. Establish: - Data user responsibilities - Training/education protocols - Usage metrics	How data will be queried and retrieved from storage and delivered to users. Establish protocols for: - Extraction - Reporting	How data will be used through dynamic and visual deployment for benchmarking, exploratory and causal analysis, and prediction and forecasting.

enterprise system, such as PeopleSoft or Banner, is the most obvious data asset, but in addition to this important system and the examples above, other assets include:

- the learning-management system (LMS);
- comparative data, including those from IPEDS (Integrated Postsecondary Education Data System), ranking publications, and other sources,
- data in vendor-based systems, such as those for recruitment, student success, assessment, or space management;
- faculty activity data;
- library data systems;

- the data warehouse(s);
- residence hall management systems;
- facilities access and energy usage data;
- network usage data;
- survey systems; and
- document imaging repositories.

The inventory may also cover external data assets that offer insight into the internal and external environment; these include:

- data feeds from social media;
- labor market demand and outcomes; and
- other real-time data that may inform strategic decision making.

At a minimum, the inventory should include the name of the asset, a brief description of the data it houses, the vendor (if applicable), the unit and person responsible for it, and the storage location of the data (university server, office file share, vendor cloud, etc.).

Activity 2: Prioritization

Once an inventory is well populated, the next step is to establish a process to prioritize integration into the data infrastructure. Just as an effective IT governance system includes an agreed-upon process for prioritizing technology projects to allocate resources to meet the most important organizational goals and needs (Weill and Ross, 2004), an effective data strategy delineates which data assets in the inventory should receive attention first. The institution's mission, goals, and strategic objectives should guide the prioritization process. For instance, a university strategically targeting improvements in undergraduate student success may place priority on the enterprise resource planning (ERP) system and the LMS system to understand how progress through course-level experiences informs degree progress, while deferring action on data assets for advancement and research. The personnel involved in setting priorities for data integration should understand the strategic goals of the institution as well as the potential for various data assets to advance these priorities.

Activity 3: Capture

For each data asset, the data strategy should identify current and optimal capture procedures. Data may be manually keyed by employees or students; optically scanned from documents or barcodes; and/or manually or automatically imported from other sources. In practice, many systems use multiple data capture methods.

For instance, undergraduate applications data may be sent to an institution from the Common Application through a direct feed, while medical records are optically scanned by staff in the health center, and current address and contact information is manually keyed by each student. As systems of capture mature, they rely more on an application programming interface (API) that feeds data directly to an institutional system and do not require the attention of employees except to ensure that they execute as scheduled. More mature systems also re-use data by transporting information that has already been captured in one system into another that requires the same entries.

Activity 4: Storage

The data strategy should identify current and optimal storage areas for each data asset. The current locations of the enterprise system for student records, the LMS, and other major systems are well known to IT professionals and can be identified easily. Data assets maintained by individual units may be less well known or defined.

For example, the institutional research (IR) office may manage its own warehouse or storage system for IPEDS unit records and benchmark data, and it may preserve external data sourced from ranking publications or environmental scans only on an ad hoc basis in a file share. In instances like these, the current location of the IR file share should be recorded, and an optimal location identified; possibilities include the institutional data warehouse, a data lake, or a location where a federated analytics system could access the file share and integrate it with other data assets.

As a result of the prioritization process, the optimal location will not always be the most integrated option for storage, but rather the option that will best advance organizational goals in an environment where resources are limited. Considerations about access may influence where data may be stored, as in the case of financial aid records received directly from the Free Application for Federal Student Aid (FAFSA), restricted-use license data for federal sample surveys, and other data assets that are subject to data use agreements.

Activity 5: Linkage

The data strategy should identify current and optimal procedures to connect each data asset to others belonging to the institution. Articulation of how data assets do and should connect with each other is context dependent, based upon existing organizational architecture and priorities. A range of current and optimal approaches to linkage will emerge, from a manual Open

Database Connectivity (ODBC) connection between a file share and a desktop workspace to automated extract, load, and transform (ELT) procedures that move data in real time into a data lake or structured repository.

Specifics about how data assets are connected should include the amount of data involved, the frequency of transfer, and the level of automation. As illustrated in Figure 2.1, dimensions of automation, frequency of transfer, and data quantity exist on a multi-dimensional spectrum. As connections require more data elements, more automation, and more currency, more monetary and IT resources will be required to implement and maintain them.

For example, a residence life operation that runs on a separate housing management system may push account charges and local addresses to the enterprise system on a nightly basis and pull demographic data back into the housing system using an API. Such a linkage constitutes a daily two-way automated transfer of limited data elements, and may be perfectly sufficient to conduct business. However, if institutional goals to improve student success mean prioritizing an examination of the effects of roommates and room changes on academic performance, then additional data elements may need to be pushed to the enterprise system or other systems to determine the relative importance of these factors.

The optimal state may thus involve increasing the amount of data flowing into the enterprise system or constructing an analytical architecture that can connect to the entirety of both systems in real time. In advancing a data strategy, it is important to resist the impulse to immediately connect everything to everything else and instead prioritize those connections that will produce early returns.

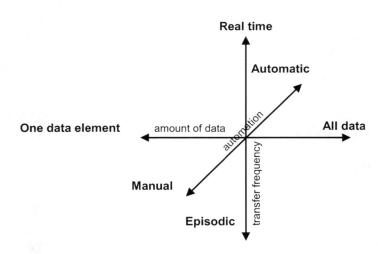

FIGURE 2.1 Key Elements of a Data Strategy

KEY ELEMENTS OF A DATA STRATEGY

A mature data architecture will integrate a majority of administrative data assets and will illustrate how reporting and analytics will connect to these assets (Campbell, Smith, and Kumar, 2018).

Activity 6: Curation

For each data asset, the data strategy should identify how data will be updated and maintained to preserve value. Data elements do not maintain themselves; a group of professionals and processes maintain them to ensure that users receive high-quality data. The data strategy should identify who is responsible for updating and maintaining data.

Further, it is useful to articulate what systems are in place to ensure the appropriate delivery of data. This may involve a series of error checks or audits or an automated notification of a completed or uncompleted process. It may also involve more detailed business analysis and communication with vendors or data providers to understand changes in data acquisition, including data feeds, definitions, cycle time, measurement point or other salient information.

DATA GOVERNANCE

Data governance formalizes behavior around the definition, production, storage, usage, and destruction of data to enable and enhance organizational effectiveness. Importantly, data governance is about people and business processes more than it is about data, and while IT professionals should participate in data governance, it should not be relegated to or led by an institution's IT unit. Further, development of effective data governance is a sufficiently complex initiative that has received extensive treatment by multiple authors (Bhansali, 2014; Seiner, 2014), and our discussion here is necessarily limited.

That said, some essential elements of data governance deserve attention. Otto (2011) notably identifies three characteristics of data governance systems: (1) connection to the organization's formal and functional goals; (2) decision making rights; and (3) roles and committees. It is also significant that the "formal" nature of data governance requires that all three of these features be documented in written form and preferably made broadly available throughout the organization, such as by posting them on a website or intranet.

Translating to a Higher Education Context

In translating these characteristics to a higher education data strategy, the data governance approach should be articulated for each data asset to include: (1) a designated decision making body with established rules for how it makes decisions about data; (2) individuals to provide data stewardship for various assets;

21

and (3) a system that produces and maintains formal (written) data dictionaries that store metadata. Colleges and universities may deem it desirable to establish a data governance system that encompasses all their data assets, although the complexity of any given institution may render a unified system impractical. For instance, a university with significant medical and hospital services may wish to govern patient data protected by the Health Insurance Portability and Accountability Act (HIPAA) using specialized structures and policies, rather than placing those data elements under the general purview of an institutional data governance council.

Data Stewards

Data stewards play an essential role in data governance, although many colleges and universities have no formal descriptions or written sets of expectations, activities, or deliverables for these positions. Data stewards conduct the day-to-day business of data governance and are accountable for effective control and use of data (Plotkin, 2014; Knight, 2017). Plotkin identifies five types of data steward roles: domain data stewards, business data stewards, technical data stewards, operational data stewards, and project data stewards.

Business data stewards are accountable for data within a particular area, such as a college or school run by a dean; they work with stakeholders to make recommendations on data issues, manage metadata for their area, champion stewardship, and communicate important information back to data users in their areas. Domain data stewards are responsible for widely shared areas of an institution, such as the registrar for university records or the controller for financial data; these individuals work with business data stewards to build consensus and consistency across the domain. Technical data stewards are usually IT staff; they provide expertise on applications, ETL, data stores, and other links in the information chain and are assigned by IT leadership to support data governance.

Operational data stewards provide support to business data stewards and hold campus roles like department course scheduler or unit hiring manager. They help enforce business rules for the data they use and may remediate data under their purview when needed; they may also recommend changes to improve data quality. Project data stewards are less common in higher education but may be appointed to help domain data stewards implement a specific project, such as a course-scheduling system or degree audit system.

Data stewards protect and curate the value of data assets under their purview. Specifically, they oversee management of selected data assets; participate in data governance and carry out decisions; assist in creating and maintaining data dictionaries and metadata; document and update rules, standards, and procedures relevant to their area of responsibility; ensure data quality and manage specific issues; communicate appropriate use and changes; and manage access and security (Stanford, 2012). These responsibilities are not trivial, and stating them explicitly in job descriptions and performance expectations can help ensure that they are properly valued and carried out.

Data Dictionaries

The responsibility for maintaining data dictionaries carries particular importance because effective use of data requires a shared "common understanding of the meaning and descriptive characteristics of that data" (International Standards Organization, 2004). An organization may be streamlined enough to adopt a systematic master data management (MDM) protocol that centralizes definitions of all data elements in a master data dictionary. But the proliferation of data assets, including those from third parties, may require the data governance body to set data dictionary standards and distribute management of the dictionaries themselves to data asset managers. For instance, Stony Brook University's data dictionary standards include a set of principles and required elements (data store, table name, data element, data element name, definition, source and data logic, data type and length, allowable values/parameters, semantic rules, data steward, date created, and date updated), with specific directions and examples for how to manage the data.

Data Dictionary Principles

1. Data dictionaries are designed to promote communication and production of meaning; as such dictionaries document the existence, meaning, and use of data elements.
2. Data dictionaries must be accessible to all users who enter and extract data from a data store.
3. Data stewards must actively maintain data dictionary contents, including definitions, values, and other metadata.
4. Data caretakers and users are responsible for actively using data dictionaries to correctly enter, select, and analyze data elements.
5. Data dictionaries should be reviewed on a regular schedule to ensure currency (Stony Brook University, 2017).

DATA QUALITY

In many organizations, calls for data governance and formulation of a data strategy are typically prompted by complaints about data quality. The data quality problem is often manifested when analysts produce different answers to the same question, when invalid values appear in reports, or when analysts spend inordinate amounts of time manually cleaning data before issuing reports. (These pain points are discussed in greater detail in Chapter 8 – Presidents' and Provosts' Perspectives.)

Missing Data

In some cases, these issues are definitional and can be addressed through data governance, but in others, the data sources are the culprit because of missing elements or logically impossible values populating fields, such as a Connecticut address in a New York county or an undergraduate art major housed in the law school. Statistics Canada (2002) offers a useful definition of data quality as "the state of completeness, validity, consistency, timeliness and accuracy that makes data appropriate for a specific use."

Missing data elements complicate even the simplest analytical work and can make it difficult for audiences to interpret percentages and ultimately understand findings. Further, requestor-based projects can be derailed by missing data; missing ZIP codes may prevent proper attribution of students to legislative districts and weaken advocacy efforts, or drop-out risk may be improperly modeled because of missing student activity information. Invalid or illegal values in data fields likewise complicate analysis because they require ad hoc data cleaning by the end user that is not replicable and entails a high probability of error. For all intents and purposes, data elements that are unavailable when they are needed are just an extreme case of missing data, and inaccuracies in data pose obvious problems.

Understanding Data Quality

Through an analysis of various data quality approaches, Batini et al. (2009) found that successful methods incorporate a collection of contextual information about business processes and storage practices, an assessment of the quality of extant data, and an improvement process. The contextual phase of data quality management includes understanding how business units operate, store data, and face challenges and costs arising from data quality issues. The data quality assessment phase requires a comparison of existing data to reference values from data dictionaries as well as a discussion with stakeholders about the most critical areas for attention.

In organizations where data quality management is nascent or developing, these assessments are ad hoc and reactive. In more mature data quality management systems, quality assurance measurement happens automatically and initiates reports highlighting data to be corrected. In the most advanced systems, organizations have distinct measurements of data quality across all data assets, with measures of completeness and validity across all elements, and have also implemented strong validation procedures upon acquisition of data to minimize the capture of invalid data. Approaches that incorporate error reporting can generally be developed locally, but systemic measurement of data quality across all data elements and sources generally requires a dedicated software solution or application.

The data quality improvement phase involves multiple activities, which are, in part, a function of the maturity of the institution's data management practices. Batini et al. (2009) found that organizations manage data quality effectively when they evaluate the costs of remediation, assign process and data responsibilities, identify causes of errors and appropriate remediation strategies, design and implement process controls, and monitor improvements. In terms of costs, institutions may have received lists of co-curricular high school activities from the Common Application as free-response text fields, with reported items such as "dance," "dance team," "competitive dance," "clogging," and "Irish step dancing," not to mention variations with misspellings and errant punctuation. Data cleanup of this field could be accomplished in various ways, but the costs might outweigh the benefits.

Data Stewards' Role in Data Quality

The data governance system should assign data stewards to all data assets to ensure quality control. Identification of causes of errors and appropriate remediation can be difficult to automate; such activities typically require an analyst who understands business processes and can troubleshoot why data stores reflect unexpected results. Monitoring of improvements can be done on an ad hoc basis, but in organizations with more mature data quality management processes, direct measurement of all data against reference values from dictionaries can offer compelling metrics about the effectiveness of any improvement efforts. Further, these measurement practices generally rely upon software solutions to determine the extent to which all data fields are complete and meet parameters in the dictionary, as well as to cross-validate them with other data elements.

DATA ACCESS

An institution's data strategy should establish provisions for data access:

1. to ensure accessibility – allowing authorized individuals to obtain and use data when and where necessary; and
2. to provide security – protecting privacy and preventing unauthorized use of sensitive information.

Moreover, a comprehensive data strategy will tailor accessibility and security requirements to each data asset, although establishment of an overarching framework to classify data assets for access and security protocols is helpful for streamlining purposes.

Accessibility

Data access in a closed paradigm is often conceptualized as user authentication to ensure that only authorized individuals have access to sensitive or restricted data; this principle is covered below under "Security." Conversely, accessibility in an open paradigm extends data out to these authorized users so that they have data when and where they need it. Considerations include the devices and networks on which data may be accessed, the applications that may be used to work with the data, and the timeliness of data. Institutional needs must be balanced with security demands as well as potential return on investment.

For instance, if a college president wishes to access her executive dashboard via her tablet using a 4G network, then use of unit-record data with personally identifiable information (e.g., student IDs or grades) as the architectural foundation of the dashboard may pose security concerns. In another instance, an enrollment manager may want real-time access to registration numbers to monitor progress toward enrollment and retention goals but may have to settle for receiving the figures nightly via the data warehouse if the cost or security limitations of obtaining them directly from the live student-information system are too significant. The data strategy should balance the data vision and institutional goals against costs and potential return. Further, since security restrictions may place additional limits on some data assets but not others, accessibility may be asset-specific.

Security

Data security in the data strategy should incorporate both an institutional approach and an asset-based approach. At the institutional level, colleges and universities already have to comply with federal laws pertaining to the handling of education records under the Family Education Rights and Privacy Act (FERPA), financial records under the Gramm-Leach-Bliley Act (GLBA), and, potentially, health records under the Health Insurance Portability and Accountability Act (HIPAA). GLBA in particular has provisions requiring institutions to maintain a formal information security program and designate an employee to coordinate it. In 2016, the Department of Education issued a Dear Colleague Letter (GEN-16–12) reminding institutions that compliance with GLBA is a requirement of their Program Participation Agreements in Title IV student aid programs and also strongly encouraging institutions to adopt protocols outlined in NIST SP 800–171 for protecting "controlled unclassified information" (Ross et al., 2015).

At the institutional level, the data security program should certainly comply with GLBA, although for many colleges and universities the protocols set forth in NIST SP 800–171 will be aspirational. From a data strategy perspective, institutions need to establish security policies that classify sensitive information, specify responsibilities of users, and include provisions for authorization protocols. The following are two strong examples:

Stanford University

The Administrative Guide's chapter on computing contains specific policies on information security, including information sensitivity, stewardship, access, and authentication protocols. See especially subchapters 6.3.1 (Information Security) and 6.4.1 (Identification and Authentication Systems). *Stanford University (2017)*

University of Michigan

Safely Use Sensitive Data are a website that details data classification levels, methods to protect sensitive data, and what kinds of data are allowable in various university systems.

Michigan (2018)

Many institutions have established a chief information security officer (CISO) position reporting to the chief information officer or at times to the president or the board, but the organization and staffing models are less important than ensuring that the function is carried out and that sufficient policies are established (Pomerantz and Grama, 2017). Additionally, the General Data Protection Regulation issued by the European Union has prompted many colleges and universities to establish more intentional and unified privacy policies. Data security and individual privacy are related but distinct concepts, and larger institutions may wish to consider the utility of a chief privacy officer as personal data proliferate.

The mere existence of institutional policies that establish levels of information sensitivity and access protocols is not enough, however; each data asset must be assigned these classifications and protocols. The University of Michigan's practice of centrally maintaining them and communicating them via a website is a leading example of how to accomplish this. A sound data strategy will also incorporate these protocols beyond centrally managed assets to those managed by units or federated into analytical networks. Restrictions on some federal financial aid data, such as information reported to institutions via FAFSA, for instance, prevent linking many of these data elements with more broadly accessible analytical databases. Therefore, institutions must take care to ensure that appropriate security and privacy protocols are maintained for each data asset and element while pursuing a strategy of broader data integration.

DATA LITERACY AND USAGE

An institutional data strategy should establish a plan to ensure that the people who regularly work with data understand what it means, can explain both its proper uses and its limitations, and can use it to support decision making and to improve operational effectiveness. This aspect of the data strategy involves setting competencies and providing sufficient professional development and on-board explanations to ensure that users are able to use data appropriately. Organizations are increasingly finding that employees do not have the data skills they need (Harris, 2012; Bradford, 2018). Especially in larger distributed environments with broad access to "democratized data" through analytics, these systems for data literacy have to be web-based to scale them sufficiently. Again, they may also need to be specific to the data asset, as in the case of the University of Washington Business Intelligence Portal Tour (2018).

Additionally, formalized policies can assist with advancing data literacy, for example by requiring job postings and position descriptions to include relevant data competencies. Establishing a formal policy for user responsibilities can also be valuable; a statement in the Stony Brook University Data Governance Framework (2016) establishes user responsibilities to "recognize that institutional data and information derived from it are potentially complex," include source information when distributing data, guard against potential misinterpretation, respect individual privacy, maintain security standards, and report data quality issues to data stewards.

Closing the loop to measure usage should start with metrics of report usage and access, but should not end there. The most basic way to gauge usage is often simply to review which reports are accessed the most. Valuable information can be gleaned about what is working in an analytics system and, perhaps more importantly, what is not. When a report or dashboard goes unused, it is often because users either don't know the tool exists or don't know how to interpret the data contained therein. In some instances, redesign and better communication can solve these issues, but it may well be that users need more training, especially with closing the loop. Ransbotham, Kiron, and Prentice (2015) found an increasing gap between the sophistication of analytics and the ability of managers to interpret and use the results. Indeed, the largest corporate challenge is not producing results but rather translating results into action. More sophisticated measures of how users understand and put data to use can take the form of short follow-up surveys asking two or three straightforward questions, such as "To what extent did the data delivered meet your needs?" (Likert scale) or "What decision or action was made based on the data?" (short free response).

DATA EXTRACTION AND REPORTING

While the acquisition provision of the data strategy covers how to get data into institutional systems, the extraction and reporting component formalizes how to query and retrieve data from storage and deliver it to users through both regular and ad hoc reporting to support day-to-day operations. Methods for querying and extracting data from storage should be identified, along with user types associated with each extraction method. The data strategy should establish roles for users who access raw data, build reports, or simply access reports.

Some personnel, such as financial aid and institutional research staff, will need direct access to data storage areas to extract large data sets with different parameters. This level of direct access through a virtual private network (VPN), secure file transfer protocol (SFTP), or other secure transfer protocol will need to be planned and established. Staff in IT or business intelligence (BI) units who build reports for other campus users will need similar access as well as a means to deliver reports securely to these constituencies. Finally, general campus users will require a way to access these reports.

For established university systems, such as the student records system or financial system, these protocols are likely already in place. A university will need to consider how to incorporate similar extraction protocols for all of the other data assets in its inventory. In most cases, the ways in which data may be extracted from the student records system will differ substantively from those used for the learning-management system (LMS), the faculty information system, or even the data warehouse. The data strategy should articulate these differences and assess the value and intentionality of each system of data extraction.

Reporting, which is distinct from analytics (see "Data Analytics"), is "the process of organizing data into informational summaries in order to monitor how different areas of a business are performing" (Dykes, 2010). Reporting represents a basic operational function and often involves lists or very simple statistics, such as counts and averages. Class rosters, lists of students on probation or suspension, daily counts of students registering before the start of the term, and statistics produced for compliance purposes such as IPEDS are all examples of the kinds of reports that systems should be designed to prepare.

The data strategy should establish principles to guide the unit or units that build and deliver reports, including those that may assemble data from distinct data assets. Among these should be a provision that reports must support operational objectives. That is, a report should be designed to accomplish a specific task, and this task should be clearly stated in the report. For example, a class roster could include a description such as "This class roster is designed for instructors to know which students are officially registered for their class section as of the date the roster is prepared. Please report discrepancies to the Registrar."

Additionally, the data strategy should establish a searchable inventory of reports and their intended use, and the inventory should be maintained in an accessible area. Reports should be automated, based on return on investment that includes some forecasting about the stability of the environment or reporting needs. Finally, the data strategy should institute some metrics for report usage, such as how often each report is run and how many distinct users run a report in a given time period. Just as with data literacy, occasional user surveys to assess what decisions are made based on reports can provide invaluable insights into how much reports contribute to the accomplishment of institutional objectives.

DATA ANALYTICS

Analytics describe the past (descriptive analytics), explain the present (exploratory analytics), forecast the future (predictive analytics), and propose future courses of action (prescriptive analytics). Data analytics are the tools and output of data analysis. In many ways, such tools have always been employed by colleges and universities. However, advances in computing power and the proliferation of digital records have led to rapid development in analytics.

Contemporary analytics offer speed, ease of use, interactivity, and utility for decision making. Moreover, they increasingly include machine-learning approaches and deployment of artificial intelligence. Analytics have also been integrated into data systems, so that room-scheduling systems, donor management systems, faculty information systems, and the like, all include their own data analytics using some level of visualization and forecasting. This reality of multiple analytics systems native to specific data assets renders the development of a coherent analytics strategy complex.

The data strategy should establish a plan for data analytics for each data asset, and for the institution as a whole, and set priorities for the integration of data assets into the institutional analytics system. The data strategy should acknowledge that a successful analytics system requires maturity in other aspects of the data strategy, including data acquisition, governance, quality, access, usage, and extraction. The analytics integration should be designed with key questions in mind that will advance the institution's strategic priorities; these often involve revenue generation, cost containment, and risk mitigation.

Examples of common descriptive and exploratory analyses appear in Table 2.2. The data strategy should identify preferred analytics systems for particular questions

KEY ELEMENTS OF A DATA STRATEGY

Table 2.2 Examples of Analytics Outputs

	Revenue Generation	Cost Containment	Risk Mitigation
Descriptive/Exploratory	Revenue per credit hour Revenue per program Application pool analysis Revenue per recruitment event	Cost per credit hour Class size distribution and optimization Space utilization Faculty workload Unit staffing per service levels Cost per service delivery	Compliance monitoring Budgeted vs. actual expenses Cost as percent of family income
	Student Success Factors	**Administrative**	
Predictive/Prescriptive	Individual predictions for: - Student grade point average - Likelihood of on-time graduation - Likelihood of attrition - Likelihood to register for a class Individual prescriptions for: - Low-impact interventions (nudges) - Medium/high-impact interventions	Faculty progress toward tenure Forecast of research productivity Forecast of department/program ranking Course demand Enrollment projections Revenue/cost forecasts	

or analyses. For instance, the analytics native to the faculty information system may be the preferred source for understanding faculty research productivity and impact but should not be used as a source for official counts of faculty members and their demographics.

DATA TOOLS

While recognizing that multiple data tools will likely play a part in its overall execution, the data strategy should identify those preferred for specific institutional functions. Acceptance of multiple tools is necessary since: (1) new tools are developed increasingly rapidly, driving innovation and reducing acquisition costs; (2) users prefer specific products and have tool-specific expertise; (3) some data assets require use of specific tools; and (4) the relative strengths and weaknesses of various data tools should prompt users to select the tool that best matches the requirements at hand.

For instance, a small college may find that it can limit statistical applications to a single package such as SAS, but mid-size and larger institutions will almost certainly need additional applications, including SPSS, R, and Stata, to support academic and research missions as well as to leverage the application-specific expertise of different analysts. Tool selection should generally follow identification of key functional questions and an assessment of local resources for deployment and analysis. Considerations should include speed, ease of use, capabilities for analysis, support for training and professional development among employees, deployment on premises or in the cloud, and capacities to access to multiple data assets.

Data tools or services are available to support any of the seven key elements of the data strategy described in this chapter. Four areas deserve special attention here: (1) storage and integration; (2) reporting; (3) business intelligence; and (4) advanced analytics. These four functions exist on a continuum moving data from various sources and transform the data into intelligence, and many tools include components of each, with some vendors offering full vertical integration of all four functions.

Further, as the marketplace for these applications and services is evolving rapidly, the examples provided here are necessarily a snapshot of the market at a point in time. Storage and integration tools may employ traditional data warehousing with extract-transform-load (ETL) procedures into a server environment on premises, such as Microsoft SQL Server. Alternatively, many larger institutions have begun to develop a data lake following an extract-load-transform (ELT) model from source data to the cloud, using Amazon Web Services, IBM Cloud, or Google Cloud Platform (Aldridge, 2018; Campbell, Smith, and Kumar, 2018). Such implementations are typically resource intensive, and the data strategy should outline the institutional approach to this level of architecture.

By and large, reporting tools act as a layer on top of the enterprise warehouse, data marts, or data lake, and again typically entail an institutional decision to support a single or limited number of approaches for data extraction and reporting. MS SQL Server Reporting Services, Crystal Reports, and Cognos are all commonly used reporting applications. BI applications have become widespread, and the market is in flux. Leaders in higher education include Tableau, Microsoft BI, and Oracle OBIEE. As Baier et al. (2018) observe in an evaluation of 20 BI platforms, Tableau provides a user-friendly platform that lowers barriers to adoption among analysts, while Microsoft's platform requires more technical skill but is more economical.

Advanced analytics involve computing approaches that generally exceed the capabilities of BI tools. Python, R, and other base tools may play a role in the analytics space, and may be integrated into more specialized applications, such as Rapid Insight, SAS Enterprise Miner, SPSS Data Modeler, or KNIME. These applications typically conduct the computationally intensive work of prediction, simulation, and forecasting, with results being disseminated either through these tools or through the BI tool layer.

FINAL THOUGHTS

Developing a data strategy is a daunting task, but articulating plans for each key element listed here can be a fruitful approach. It must be remembered that creating and implementing a data strategy is not an IT project but rather a systemic process for an organization. Development of the strategy should be inclusive, not only to harness institutional priorities and knowledge but also to garner buy-in from key constituencies.

As it evolves, the strategy should be articulated formally and published, at least for institutional consumption. If the organization's data strategy is not written down and communicated, then it is not a strategy, it is a secret. Finally, institutions must anticipate the need to devote resources to the data strategy and infrastructure. Sustainable systemic processes that transform an organization generally cannot be supported as distributed assignments on top of existing personnel and functions.

The importance of adopting a data strategy likely cannot be overestimated. Gartner (2017) says that within five years organizations will be valued on their information portfolios. Higher education institutions already compete in this environment for students, dollars, time, and political and social positioning. The institutions that most effectively and intentionally adapt to the new reality of pervasive data will establish a competitive advantage through strategic curation and leveraging of data capital that will create opportunities not unlike financial capital does today.

DISCUSSION QUESTIONS

1. List the major data assets of your organization. To what extent are they integrated with each other, and how does this reflect current institutional priorities and future institutional needs?
2. Recognizing that the formulation of a data strategy should not fall solely to IT but should instead be led by functional operations; who should be involved in developing the data strategy and monitoring its effectiveness?
3. How will the effectiveness of the data strategy be assessed? What metrics should be established for each part of the strategy, and who will be responsible for collecting and evaluating them?

4. How do data security considerations change as more people are involved in creating and implementing a data strategy?
5. Consider the maturity of your institution in each of the key elements in a data strategy. Which is the element that your institution needs to focus on the most and why? What challenges are you anticipating with the element and what are strategies to mitigate those challenges?

REFERENCES

Aldridge, B. (2018). Lead the charge: CSU's transformational data program. Educause Annual Conference, Denver, CO. Retrieved Nov. 28, 2018 from https://events.educause.edu/annual-conference/2018/agenda/lead-the-charge-transformational-data-leadership.

Baier, L., et al. (2018). BARC score enterprise BI and analytics platforms. Retrieved Nov. 28, 2018 from https://media.bitpipe.com/io_14x/io_144396/item_1786174/2018-07-16-barc_score_enterprise_bi_and_analytics_platforms_fin_ASL12447USEN.pdf

Batini, C., et al. (2009). Methodologies for data quality assessment and improvement. *ACM Computing Surveys 41*(3) Article 16, 1–50.

Bhansali, N., ed. (2014). *Data governance: Creating value from information assets.* Boca Raton, FL: CRC Press, Taylor & Francis Group.

Bradford, L. (2018, Oct. 11). Why all employees need data skills in 2019 (and beyond). *Forbes.* Retrieved Mar. 18, 2019 from www.forbes.com/sites/laurencebradford/2018/10/11/why-all-employees-need-data-skills-in-2019-and-beyond/#1ea80b65510f

British Library. (2017). *Data strategy 2017.* Retrieved July 16, 2018 from https://blogs.bl.uk/files/britishlibrarydatastrategyoutline.pdf

Campbell, J., Smith, K., and Kumar, T. (2018). Building and analytics infrastructure in-house. Association of Public and Land-Grant Universities Annual Meeting, New Orleans, LA. Retrieved Nov. 24, 2018 from www.aplu.org/members/commissions/information-measurement-analysis/cima-presentations-2018/In-House%20data%20infastructure.pdf

Carruthers, C. and Jackson, P. (2018). *The chief data officer's playbook.* London: Facet.

Dykes, B. (2010). Reporting vs. analysis: What's the difference? Retrieved Oct. 5, 2018 from https://theblog.adobe.com/reporting-vs-analysis-whats-the-difference

Gartner (2017). www.gartner.com/en/newsroom/press-releases/2017-02-08-gartner-says-within-five-years-organizations-will-be-valued-on-their-information-portfolios

Harris, J. (2012) Data are useless without the skills to analyze it. *Harvard Business Review*. Retrieved Oct. 1, 2018 from https://hbr.org/2012/09/data-is-useless-without-the-skills

Hosch, B. (2017). Beyond data governance to data strategy. Annual Forum of the Association for Institutional Research, Washington, DC.

Kiron, D. (2017). Lessons from becoming a data-driven organization. *MIT Sloan Management Review 58*(2), 3–13.

Knight, M. (2017). What is data stewardship? Retrieved Oct. 15, 2018 from www.dataversity.net/what-is-data-stewardship

Levy, E. (2018). 5 essential components of a data strategy. SAS Whitepaper. Retrieved Oct. 1, 2018 from www.sas.com/content/dam/SAS/en_us/doc/whitepaper1/5-essential-components-of-data-strategy-108109.pdf

Otto, B. (2011). A morphology of the organisation of data governance. ECIS 2011 Proceedings 272. http://aisel.aisnet.org/ecis2011/272.

Plotkin, D. (2014). *Data stewardship: An actionable guide to effective data management*. Waltham, MA: Morgan Kaufmann.

Pomerantz, J. and Grama, J. (2017). IT leadership in higher education, 2016: The chief information security officer. Research report. Louisville, CO: ECAR. Retrieved Sept. 13, 2018 from https://library.educause.edu/~/media/files/library/2017/7/ers1702ciso.pdf

Ransbotham, S., Kiron, D., and Prentice, P. (2015). Minding the analytics gap. *MIT Sloan Management Review 56*, 63–68.

Ross, R. et al. (2015). Protecting controlled unclassified information in nonfederal information systems and organizations. National Institutes of Standards and Technology Special Publication 800-171. Retrieved Sept. 13, 2018 from http://dx.doi.org/10.6028/NIST.SPP.800-171

Seiner, R. S. (2014). *Non-invasive data governance: The path of least resistance and greatest success*. Basking Ridge, NJ: Technics Publications.

Stanford University. (2012). Responsibilities related to data stewardship. Retrieved Oct. 15 from www.stanford.edu/dept/pres-provost/cgi-bin/dg/wordpress/wp-content/uploads/2012/01/DG-Data-Stewardship.doc.

Stanford University. (2017). *Administrative guide: Chapter 6 computing*. Retrieved Sept. 13, 2018 from https://adminguide.stanford.edu/chapter-6

Statistics Canada. (2002). *Statistics Canada's quality assurance framework – 2002*. Statistics Canada Catalogue no. 12-586-XIE.

Stony Brook University. (2016). *Data governance framework at Stony Brook University*. Retrieved Oct. 1, 2018 from www.stonybrook.edu/commcms/irpe/about/_files/DataGovFramework.pdf.

Stony Brook University. (2017). *Data dictionary standards.* Retrieved Sept. 6, 2018 from www.stonybrook.edu/commcms/irpe/about/data_governance/_files/DataDictionaryStandards.pdf

University of Michigan. (2018). Safely use sensitive data. Retrieved Sept. 13, 2018 from www.safecomputing.umich.edu/protect-the-u/safely-use-sensitive-data.

University of Washington. (2018). BI portal tour. Retrieved Oct. 1, 2018 from http://itconnect.uw.edu/work/data/bi-portal-intro

Weill, P. and Ross, J. (2004). *IT governance: How top performers manage IT decision rights for superior results.* Boston, MA: Harvard Business School Press.

Chapter 3

Using Concepts from Strategic Planning

Angela E. Henderson and Resche D. Hines

INTRODUCTION

No strategy can succeed in the absence of planning and preparation. This is especially true of a data strategy, which may be an unfamiliar term to stakeholders. In framing this discussion, we look to strategic planning practices that have been effective in guiding institutional change. Historically, resistance to organizational change within higher education has been exacerbated by the lack of a strategic planning structure and data-driven decision making processes. The absence of these factors draws into question the dynamic between an institution's culture, politics, and ability to implement effective change-management strategies for improved performance. Most would agree that the organizational dynamics of higher education are unique and can be especially problematic in implementing a strategic planning process to drive organizational cultural change.

In addition, strategic planning has moved from the age of *Encyclopedia Britannica*-informed decision making, when information was already dated by the time it was accessible, to the Google/Alexa age, where real-time data can shape strategic planning processes. Today, the most pressing data challenge for institutions is translating the vast amounts of data available into consumable information that truly illuminates the most critical components of the planning process. To operate optimally in today's competitive higher education environment, institutions must develop interwoven processes that quickly allow data to inform strategy.

These processes, contextualized to fit each institution's strategic plan, enable institutions to leverage findings to quickly implement strategies that inform the next round of data collection. Findings also inform data strategies needed to enhance the next iteration of the strategic plan. Thus, the purpose of these interwoven processes is to implement a comprehensive strategic planning protocol nested in data and disseminated through an annual planning process that includes updating organizational and individual unit missions, goals and objectives, learning and program outcomes, assessment and evaluation, and establishment of priorities and budgeting. The development and implementation of these strategic activities help both to align the institution's strategic and data planning processes to the vision and core values of the institution and to inform internal and external stakeholders.

Institutions must be dedicated to enhancing planning efforts. Therefore, they must understand and balance organizational context with the implementation and support of planning guidelines; management guidelines; resource allocation; and identification of goals, outcomes, and measures. This balance facilitates real-time relevant and meaningful data-informed effectiveness indicators and allows for broad-based involvement from key institutional stakeholders. These processes assist the institution in maintaining accreditation, promoting achievement of its mission, and fostering continual enhancement of the institution's programs and services for the benefit of the institutional community. The foundation for developing such an informed and effective strategic planning process is data. Institutions must strive to develop data structures and strategies that facilitate sound data use and stewardship. The challenge faced by higher education is no longer a lack of timely data, but rather how to develop data practices that effectively and efficiently utilize institutional resources.

In the competitive environment of higher education, it is critical for an institution to utilize every possible advantage. Developing a data strategy through a collaborative, data-driven strategic planning framework allows an institution to examine its current position with an eye toward beneficial and attainable improvement.

CORE ELEMENTS OF STRATEGIC PLANNING AND APPLICATION TO DATA STRATEGY

Strategic planning, by definition, comprises two key elements: a strategy and a plan. A plan is simply a method for achieving an end. *Merriam-Webster's* defines strategy primarily as "the science and art of employing the political, economic, psychological, and military forces of a nation or group of nations to afford the maximum support to adopted policies in peace or war" (Strategy, n.d.). Although this definition is somewhat militaristic in tone, it is not entirely out of place in higher education, where numerous factions are competing for resources. With just a few modifications, we develop a definition of strategy more applicable to higher education: the science and art of employing cultural, political, economic, environmental, and psychological forces of *an institution* to afford the maximum support to proposed and adopted priorities.

As Allison and Kaye (2015) noted, strategy and planning fundamentally differ in nature: "strategy is aspirational in setting direction and is focused on broad, fundamental choices. Planning involves translating the strategy into concrete goals and guidance for how to achieve them" (p. 2). Even the most successful leader cannot singlehandedly drive a strategic plan; only a combination of planning, strategy, and data will work. The gap between aspirational position and concrete goals must be bridged by data for a strategic plan to be successful.

Although the role of data in the planning process is often not explicitly articulated, data are a critical and foundational component of the planning process. Aspirational strategy must be grounded in data, just as planning goals must be data-driven. This reality tends to be overlooked or minimized; however, when data does not inform and drive the plan, organizations often experience difficulty sustaining strategic planning processes. Without all three elements in balance (as shown in Figure 3.1), the process often fails; although some degree of success might be attained, none of the elements work effectively in isolation. When data flows through the process to both inform and evaluate, the elements are integrated properly to drive action.

As noted in Chapter 1, a data strategy is similar to a strategic plan in that it "brings together data collection and analysis elements throughout the entire organization into one unified plan and set of goals." Given that data are an integral component of the strategic planning process, it makes sense for a data strategy to be developed according to similar principles. Correspondingly, care should be taken to avoid the type of negative perceptions often associated with strategic planning. Specifically, a data strategy should be grounded in the operational practices of the institution, based on input from a broad range of individuals, and transparent in communication of its purpose and potential impact.

As discussed in the following section, many of the considerations and processes used to guide the development of a strategic plan can be used in the development of a data strategy. Establishing a data strategy can be a complex undertaking; institutions are wise to leverage existing strategic planning infrastructure and expertise whenever possible.

FIGURE 3.1 Foundational Planning Components

FIGURE 3.2 Summary of Planning Processes

Figure 3.2 illustrates the relationship between the key components of a strategic plan; each of these elements is discussed in detail below, along with its application to data strategy.

LEADERSHIP

Strategic Planning

The strategic planning process is typically shepherded either by a designated chief planning officer (CPO) or by an appointed committee. As strategic planning impacts the entire institution, leadership tends to be distributed across multiple divisions, departments, and stakeholders. This diverse structure ensures that strategic plan priorities are informed by perspectives representing all areas of the institution. The CPO or the chair of the strategic planning committee is responsible not only for guiding the development of the plan but also for monitoring progress toward priority goals. In this capacity, leadership should demonstrate institutional support both verbally and materially, through investment of substantial resources to support planning priorities. Leaders must also be willing to question existing methods, processes, and procedures, and to push to expand systems.

Data Strategy

Whereas an individual with a formal chief planning officer title often guides the strategic planning process, few institutions (if any) have a designated data strategy officer. Although the CPO could lead the development of a data strategy, the intricacies of the various data ownership and structure issues might be challenging if the CPO is unfamiliar with the institution's data. While strategic planning is perceived as an institution-wide process with distributed ownership, data strategy is narrower in focus, directly affecting only those departments responsible for different data facets. As data ownership is dispersed across the institution, oversight of a data strategy process becomes more nebulous.

Centralized and Decentralized Models

There are two distinct methods of leadership that might be employed in pursuit of a data strategy: centralized and decentralized. The approach that works best is contingent on institutional structure and culture. In a centralized model, strong leadership is essential, especially as the concept of a data strategy is relatively new to many. Leadership must be able not only to articulate why a data strategy is important to the institution, but also to encourage participation from the numerous data-using entities across campus. Given the scope of the tasks and complexity of the relationships involved, a diffuse leadership structure with representatives from multiple areas is more likely to be successful.

Consider the structure of a faculty senate body: the shared function of teaching brings together faculty members from diverse colleges, disciplines, and levels to address curricular and academic issues that affect the institution overall. Institutions can mirror this structure to develop a data senate in which the shared function of working with data brings together individuals from diverse divisions, departments, and levels to address data-related issues that affect the institution. Just as not every faculty member is a part of the faculty senate, not everyone who works with data needs to participate in the data senate; however, there should be representation from each of the key data areas within the institution. Building a data senate group with representatives who can effectively advocate for different areas is critical. As a starting point, consider initiating a core leadership team with representatives from key data areas such as Admissions, Financial Aid, Registrar, Information Technology, Institutional Research, Student Success, Human Resources, and Finance. Without input from these multiple stakeholders, a data strategy is incomplete and unlikely to be successful.

In a decentralized leadership model, every unit within the institution becomes responsible for implementing and assessing unit-level goals in support of the institution's overall commitment to the data strategy. Employing a decentralized planning approach distributes the responsibility for building a data strategy across all departments rather than to a formal committee with the potential to be perceived as embodying an institutional response to outside pressures. The increased collaboration inherent in a decentralized model also promotes awareness of the interdependent nature of the various departments and the impact that their respective actions can have on the institution overall (Hickman, 2010).

Therefore, a decentralized system not only empowers individuals responsible for departmental planning, but also provides "freedom for the leader to focus on broader strategic issues rather than primarily day-to-day management" (Offerman, 2010, p. 192). The benefits are not limited to leaders; newly empowered staff often experience higher levels of motivation and satisfaction, resulting in higher morale and productivity across the campus (Offerman, 2010). This shared responsibility also helps alleviate the perception that data strategy goals exist solely in response to external pressures and will fade in time.

MISSION, VISION, AND VALUES

Strategic Planning

The mission statement defines the primary purpose of the institution and should thus serve as the foundation for the entire strategic plan. Plans that are at odds with the mission statement are unlikely to be supported by stakeholders, making success unlikely. Similarly, the plan should adhere to the vision and values of the institution. A strong strategic plan will help an institution attain its vision while supporting its values. As Hinton (2012) suggested, the mission and vision represent the two ends of the spectrum of institutional status: the current status and the anticipated future status. The strategic plan serves as a conduit from the former to the latter.

Alignment to institutional mission and vision is critical for success. Leadership should conduct a review of the mission and vision prior to the development of the strategic plan to ensure that an appropriate foundation for alignment exists.

Data Strategy

A sound data strategy should align with the strategic plan and, by extension, the mission, vision, and values of the institution, even if those connections are not explicitly stated. A successful data strategy supports the strategic plan through improved data structures and data-informed decision making that inherently promote the attainment of institutional goals.

Proper alignment of unit goals with the campus mission and strategic plan creates support for initiatives that advance the institution, rather than for short-term actions. Integration of these long-term initiatives demonstrates to the campus community that the strategic use of data yields benefits for the university as a whole through increased enrollments, research opportunities, and endowments.

Despite intentional alignment and potential gains, some resistance to organizational change is inevitable. Resistance can take multiple forms: chiefly, denial of the justification for change, refusal to assume responsibility for change, refusal to implement mandated activities to support change, and attempts to undo steps that have been taken toward attaining change (Agocs, 1997). Institutions can seek to diminish resistance through intentional communications, strong relationships with stakeholders, and clearly articulated goals.

COMMUNICATION

Strategic Planning

With a strong alignment foundation in place, the next step in developing a strategic plan is typically a series of carefully crafted communications to campus stakeholders detailing institutional commitment to the planning process and providing information on upcoming opportunities to give feedback. These communications should include concrete data on the potential gains to be realized from the strategic plan, such as increased enrollments, expansion of the faculty body, increased diversity, and additional revenue streams, as well the potential impact of not changing (i.e., what each scenario means in terms of resources, budgets, quality, etc.). This step is critical, as research has shown (Davidson, 2011) that stakeholders who understand the rationale for changes and the potential long-term benefits are more likely to commit their support.

As a strategic plan has a broad impact institution-wide, its success requires involvement and input from numerous stakeholders representing diverse areas of the institution. It is not uncommon for institutions to hold open forums to generate discussion of potential topics for inclusion in a strategic plan to allow all stakeholders the opportunity to provide feedback. Since the strategic plan serves as a foundation for unit and departmental goals and actions, this broad communication is critical to ensuring a shared understanding of the institutional vision.

Data Strategy

Whereas strategic planning has become ingrained in institutions over the last few decades, few institutions have an entrenched data strategy. Consequently, targeted communication is even more critical in developing a data strategy. The term "data strategy" is likely unfamiliar to most campus stakeholders and may generate confusion and frustration if the process is perceived to be purely administrative and enacted without context. To minimize this discomfort, leadership must clearly define and communicate the purpose and goals of the data strategy.

Clear communication can help establish a culture that is receptive to developing a data strategy. As with any new process, transparency increases the likelihood of success. Stakeholders need to know not only why the process is occurring and the expected outcomes, but also how it will affect their daily operations. This is particularly critical with a data strategy in order to minimize the perception of the process as a means of administrative data control. The purpose of implementing a data strategy must be clearly communicated and reiterated frequently.

Conversely, what the data strategy is *not* should also be communicated, to provide clarity. It is not a means of seizing control of data from departments, nor a way to reduce the data workforce, nor an attempt to manipulate data. It is a means of unifying institutional data, reducing duplicative efforts, and building a stronger data foundation to inform decision making.

Fostering relationships with other campus leaders and stakeholders is also critical in this endeavor. Many decisions directly influencing the institution's planning priorities and practices are made at the departmental level. Without relationships in place to remind departments how their decisions influence the institution as a whole, units act as silos, unaware of their connections to the bigger picture.

ENVIRONMENTAL SCAN

Strategic Planning

Despite alignment with the mission and vision, some ideas generated as part of the strategic planning process may be at odds with the institutional culture. An environmental scan examines the campus climate through a variety of lenses, including "social, economic, political, regulatory, technological, and cultural" (Tromp, 2004, p. 9). Identifying potential hurdles that may arise from these areas early in the planning process helps minimize the likelihood of such issues derailing the strategic plan later.

Data Strategy

Within the context of developing a data strategy, an environmental scan must examine not only the institutional culture but also the institutional *data* culture. Whereas an environmental scan for strategic planning is broad in scope, an environmental scan for a data strategy is more focused and must take into consideration existing data systems, technologies, users, and institutional perceptions. Specific challenges likely to affect the success of the data strategy should also be identified. These might include incompatible data systems, software limitations, data quality issues, data ownership issues, or lack of support for institutional data systems. Early identification of these types of potential challenges informs goal planning and increases the likelihood of success.

GOALS, OBJECTIVES, AND ACTION STEPS

Strategic Planning

Goals are the core of the strategic plan; they articulate what the institution intends to achieve in the broadest sense. Institutions may be tempted to skip the preliminaries and jump right into goal setting, but the shared understanding of mission, vision, values, and environment gained from the prior steps is critical to the success of the plan. Similarly, creating a plan based on goals used by other colleges or universities, even peers, can be a recipe for failure. In many cases, goals are institution-specific and non-transferable. Although there are a great number of shared goals across higher education institutions (e.g., increasing enrollment and raising retention rates), each goal should be examined in light of the individual institution's mission, vision, and environment to see if it is a good fit. Goals that exist outside the official guiding mission and vision of the university generally fail to impact institutional processes and culture substantially.

Goals should be considered in light of the timeline of the strategic plan. Strategic plans range in terms of time frame, often varying from three to ten years. An institution on a three-year strategic plan will have different goals than an institution on a ten-year plan. For example, a three-year strategic plan would not include a goal to improve the six-year graduation rate, as results of changes made would not be evident for six years. Similarly, goals should be distributed across the time frame of the plan and not be concentrated near either the beginning or the end (Hinton, 2012).

Each goal contains objectives that are specific statements of what must be accomplished in order for the goal to be met. Each objective then contains action steps – detailed descriptions of the actions that must be taken to achieve the objective. Action steps specify what will be done, who will be responsible, and the time frame for accomplishment. Without a formal means of performance assessment and assigned responsibility, strategic efforts tend to founder. Initiatives undertaken in the absence of systematic accountability and alignment to institutional priorities are likely to be minimally successful at best.

Data Strategy

Goals remain at the core of the data strategy, stating what the institution intends to achieve in the broadest sense. Just as in strategic planning, objectives and action steps support the goals and provide specific statements of what must be accomplished in order for a goal to be attained. While strategic plan goals tend to address broad areas such as student success, global citizenship, or diversity, goals for a data strategy are significantly narrower in focus. Data strategy goals should incorporate specific objectives and action steps that improve institutional data functions. Ultimately, if attained, data strategy goals should affect multiple areas of the institution or institutional processes overall.

To ensure that efforts towards accomplishing data strategy initiatives are progressing appropriately, a formal means of assessment is necessary. Assessments should reflect and align with institutional priorities and academic outcomes. When possible, progress updates on data strategy initiatives should be integrated into annual unit assessment reports that demonstrate departmental goal progress in support of the institutional mission and strategic plan. Incorporating data strategy goals into established institutional effectiveness reporting systems reinforces the fact that they reflect embedded values and are not stand-alone initiatives.

Table 3.1 provides a summary comparison of the key elements outlined above.

In conclusion, at the most concise level, development of a strategic plan (or a data strategy) can be guided by five key questions (shown in Figure 3.3).

KEY DIFFERENCES FROM STRATEGIC PLANNING

Although the parallels between developing a strategic plan and a data strategy are many, there are several key differences. Perhaps foremost is the scope of input sought to inform the plan/strategy. Whereas strategic plans typically originate from broad organizational input across levels and roles, the input pool for a data strategy is more limited and focused in scope, including only those individuals knowledgeable about and actively involved with the institution's data-management processes.

This narrower scope presents both benefits and challenges. Firstly, while it may be easier to gather input from a smaller number of individuals, as the scope narrows the perception of ownership increases. A strategic plan tends to be somewhat nebulous in nature, often lacking champions willing to take ownership

Table 3.1 Summary Comparison of Strategic Planning and Data Strategy Elements

Component	Strategic Plan	Data Strategy
Leadership	Chief planning officer, strategic planning committee with broad campus representation	Data senate committee with representation from key campus data areas
Mission, Vision, and Values	Must align with the mission, vision, and values of the institution	Should align with the strategic plan, and by extension, the mission, vision, and values of the institution
Communication	Frequent campus-wide broad communications to encourage involvement and input from stakeholders representing diverse areas	Frequent targeted communication to data stakeholders to encourage understanding of the purpose and goals of the data strategy
Environmental Scan	Broad in scope; takes into consideration numerous aspects of campus climate including culture, politics, economics, and social factors	Focused in scope; takes into consideration existing data culture, data systems, technologies, and institutional perceptions
Goals, Objectives, and Action steps	Focus on broad areas such as student success, diversity, global citizenship, or distinction	Focus on specific areas related to improvement of institutional data systems and processes

---

Consider the following:

1. Who will be involved? Identify leadership and involve stakeholders who will serve as champions of the process.
2. What areas of interest are supported by the mission and vision? Identify areas that align with the mission, values, and vision and are supported by stakeholder feedback.
3. What are current environmental factors? Consider the institutional culture and evaluate potential challenges and gains.
4. Are there competing priorities? How long will it take to accomplish the determined priorities (three years, five years, ten years)? Modify the time frame of the plan accordingly.
5. How will success be defined? Define goals, objectives, and action steps that outline how the institution will attain the desired outcomes.

FIGURE 3.3 **Key Questions for Consideration**

of specific goals. Because a data strategy development group comprises individuals who are regularly involved in data processes and structures, ownership is more personal. For example, individuals from the admissions department may perceive that they have complete ownership over all aspects of data collected during the admission process.

Secondly, despite the scope of involvement, strategic planning is often perceived as something that is *done to* an organization, not something that originates organically. A data strategy, with its more limited scope of input, can be more organic in nature. Based on the shared context of institutional data, individuals within the data strategy development group can perform deeper explorations of processes and structures, allowing new concerns to arise and become part of the discussion. Data strategies should be living and breathing documents that are informed and driven by data.

Thirdly, data strategies must be more nimble than traditional strategic plans. Strategic plans, generally revised every three to five years, are focused on large-scale aspirational change. Data strategies must be more flexible in nature and adaptable to accommodate changes in technologies and user expectations. As such, timelines attributed to data strategies should be abbreviated in nature, generally spanning no more than two years.

EXISTING TECHNICAL AND ORGANIZATIONAL TOOLS

Nearly any strategic planning tool can also be useful in developing a data strategy. Several of the most effective are discussed below, namely affinity mapping, SWOT analysis, DATA analysis, and strategy updates.

Affinity Mapping

As fewer people are involved in the development of a data strategy than a strategic plan, and those who are involved have their own priorities, evaluating items for inclusion can be challenging. Allowing numerous issues to emerge from broad feedback is essential. A strong data strategy depends on a strong understanding of existing data practices at an institution. Taking a cue from the visual affinity mapping strategy used for strategic planning, institutions can employ a data mapping process.

Affinity mapping begins with individuals independently jotting down ideas or issues on Post-it notes. Each Post-it note should contain only a single idea or issue. Participants may create as many notes as desired. Once they have finished, they place the notes on a broad workspace, such as a wall or whiteboard. After all the notes have been added to the workspace, a facilitator may either independently categorize them thematically or guide the contributors through a thematic grouping of the ideas/issues. The facilitator then fosters a discussion of the themes that emerged to determine if they accurately represent the general ideas/issues brought forth by the group.

Adapting the basics of the affinity mapping process to focus on data demands creates a process that mirrors that of strategic visual mapping but with different content and outcomes. Rather than asking participants to identify actions required to attain long-term success, data strategy mapping asks them to start by identifying their data demands (as specifically as possible). Data demands might be existing demands (e.g., federally mandated retention and graduation data) or demands on the horizon. Along with each demand, participants must indicate the area they represent at the institution. These demands are collected and then clustered thematically. Keywords are selected to represent each cluster (enrollment, retention, athletics, etc.). Examination of the clusters reveals not only the topics of largest data demand but also the overlap across institutional areas that may exist within the same cluster. For example, a cluster on enrollment data may show that multiple areas are unknowingly collecting the same data on student athletes.

Identification of redundant data collection and analysis is key to developing a data strategy. This process helps an institution detect overlap in demand and ownership (Are multiple areas doing the same thing? at the same time? for different audiences?). Redundant demands should be flagged for deeper examination and discussion.

After redundancies have been identified, demands should be re-clustered by area to examine the extent to which each area is responsible for meeting the institution's data demands. Are redundancies frequent between specific areas (e.g., admissions and IR)? Where redundancies occur, is one area better suited to be the official "owner" of the data? If so, how does this shift in ownership affect the overall data contribution of the area?

SWOT Analysis

SWOT analyses are one of the most commonly used planning tools and provide a simple means of evaluating institutional circumstances. A SWOT analysis examines the strengths, weaknesses, opportunities, and threats regarding a particular situation. Typically, a SWOT analysis is organized into a quadrant grid, with one aspect placed in each of the quadrants. Limiting the amount of space for responses prompts users to identify broad issues concisely. SWOT analyses are extremely beneficial as they foster discussion not only of opportunities, but also of threats that may hinder the success of the plan or strategy. Proactive awareness of potential disruptions is critical, as many institutions fail to attain goals because they avoid dealing with disruptions that arise.

Although typically conducted in a group setting, SWOT analyses can also be completed independently or in small groups prior to joining the larger group. This type of pre-planning for the larger SWOT discussion allows participants time to brainstorm and reflect more deeply on potential opportunities and threats. Providing participants with topic prompts and a blank SWOT template alleviates the pressure to consider every aspect of every quadrant on the spot and encourages deeper analysis of the issues at hand. This approach also facilitates collection of ideas from participants who prefer to have time to process multiple aspects of an issue before responding.

DATA Analysis

Once a number of potential key data priorities are identified through a SWOT analysis, it may be beneficial to conduct a deeper analysis of each one in greater detail. Similar in nature to a SWOT analysis, a DATA analysis asks users to consider four factors to determine the viability of an identified data priority: demand, accuracy, timeliness, and advantage (as shown in Figure 3.4). Priorities that are advanced for inclusion in the data strategy should be those that rely on data in high demand, are consistently validated, and result in a benefit to the institution. Benefits may take the form of decreased duplication of efforts, a reduction in resources required, or production of data that provide a competitive advantage.

This tool presents a simplified way of examining a data priority holistically. Just as not all actions that might improve an institution can be included in a strategic plan, not all those that might improve an institution's data

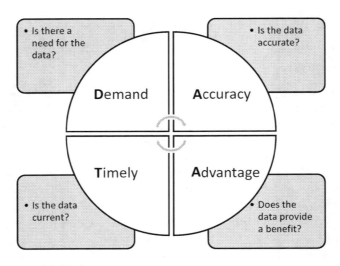

FIGURE 3.4 DATA Analysis

circumstances can be included in a data strategy. Prioritizing the items for inclusion provides a means of more quickly targeting critical needs. Although deep data issues may exist, if they are contained within a single department and only arise with the generation of a report updated every five years, actions to address them are unlikely to merit inclusion in a data strategy. Conversely, resolving a data disconnect that results in three departments duplicating efforts on a weekly basis would be a high priority, likely to yield more consistent data and a more efficient use of resources.

Strategy Updates

Strategies and plans require attention to ensure that they are progressing as desired. A simple way to integrate accountability checks is to ask for monthly updates from data strategy leaders. These brief updates should answer three questions about the data strategy: (1) what progress has been made towards the goal? (2) what challenges have been experienced?, and (3) what revisions are needed to meet the goal?

The updates should be completed monthly and shared with all individuals responsible for shepherding the institution's data strategy plan, as well as with administrative leadership to allow maximum flexibility and opportunity for insights and revisions. Updates are not meant to be onerous, but rather to ensure that the strategy stays on track and remains at the forefront of awareness. Updates allow data leaders to examine whether the strategies are working and, if they are not, to determine how they might be improved. This approach also helps combat the notion that strategic planning is inflexible and stale. Monitoring progress pulse points allows the data strategy to be nimble and relevant.

For a data strategy to be successful, leaders must strive to embed data initiatives within the day-to-day operations of the institution so that they become an incontrovertible part of the institutional culture. This will not be quickly accomplished but, as with the integration of other recent necessities such as strategic budget planning and institutional effectiveness, support and repetition will eventually produce the desired results. Just as changes in state funding and accreditation requirements prompted integrated budget planning and assessment to become a part of the institutional fabric, changing infrastructures and resources now require colleges and universities to incorporate institution-wide data strategies. True institutional investment, coupled with a willingness to implement new processes, procedures, and actions, is necessary to move a college/university towards adopting a comprehensive data strategy.

DISCUSSION QUESTIONS

1. Who (person or position) is best suited to lead a data strategy initiative at your institution?
2. Which specific departments should be represented? Are there other stakeholder groups that should be involved?
3. What type of targeted communications would be most effective at your institution?
4. How would you ensure that the data strategy aligns with the institutional mission, values, and priorities?
5. Are there cultural factors within the institution that might influence the development of the data strategy? How would these be addressed?
6. Which planning tools are likely to be effective at your institution? Why?

REFERENCES

Agocs, C. (1997). Institutionalized resistance to organizational change: Denial, inaction and repression. *Journal of Business Ethics*, *16*(9), 917–931.

Allison, M. & Kaye, J. (2015). *Strategic planning for nonprofit organizations: A practical guide for dynamic times* (3rd ed.). Hoboken, NJ: John Wiley & Sons.

Davidson, M. N. (2011). *The end of diversity as we know it: Why diversity efforts fail and how leveraging difference can succeed*. San Francisco: Berrett-Koehler Publishers.

Hickman, G. R. (2010). *Leading organizations: Perspectives for a new era* (2nd ed.). London: SAGE.

Hinton, K. E. (2012). *A practical guide to strategic planning in higher education*. Ann Arbor, MI: Society for College and University Planning.

Offerman, L. (2010). Empowerment. In Hickman, G. (Ed.), *Leading organizations: Perspectives for a new era* (2nd ed.). London: SAGE.

Strategy. (n.d.). In *Merriam-Webster Online*. Retrieved September 7, 2018 from www.merriam-webster.com/dictionary/strategy

Tromp, S. & Ruben, B. (2004). *Strategic planning in higher education: A guide for leaders*. Washington, DC: National Association of College and University Business Officers.

Chapter 4

Data Strategy versus Information Technology Planning

Sandra Kinney and Jason Lee Wang

INTRODUCTION

Information technology (IT) and data play a large part in the overall structure of an institution, affecting delivery of services, communication, academic support, compliance, and research. With the rapid evolution of technology, data strategy has become more and more crucial as institutions strive to maintain a competitive edge against one another and respond to disruptions caused by technological innovations. The changes in technology, data, and how we access data have changed dramatically in recent years. Data are being used in ways we never thought were possible. New developments in machine learning, biometrics, storage, and collection of data are occurring daily. To keep up with the rapid changes and competitive environments across higher education, IT planning must align with data strategy, but each institution must also work within the constraints of resources.

Data strategy is often confused with IT planning; however, the two are very different in concept and execution. Knowing the difference between a data strategy and an IT plan is crucial, since the two must work in conjunction with one another for successful implementation within an organization. While there are some shared components between the two, data strategy is long term and goal-oriented with a focus on a high-level course of action, while IT planning is operational and tactical in nature, with a focus on tools, people, platforms, development, budget, and approach.

This chapter identifies the core elements of both a data strategy and an IT plan, the differences between the plans, and the benefits of using both types of plans within an institution of higher education.

CORE ELEMENTS OF A DATA STRATEGY

Data Strategy Environment

A data strategy describes goals, objectives, and actions pertaining to an institution's data and the people, technology, and processes using this data. It builds upon and encompasses IT infrastructure and data governance elements, simultaneously informed by and directing the respective plans (Eckerson, 2011). A data strategy provides purposeful and data-driven direction for data acquisition, processing and integration, analytics, literacy and usage, and dissemination at a college or university. Furthermore, it formalizes data standards, practices, and procedures across the institution to ensure reliability and repeatability.

The critical characteristic of a successful data strategy is its alignment and integration with the IT plan, the data governance plan, and the institutional mission and priorities (Figure 4.1). The cohesiveness of the IT and data governance plans provides a strong foundation for the overarching goals identified in a data strategy while also setting the rules, processes, and access that support the strategic goals. This allows for a focused and consistent approach to data by all levels of data stakeholders at the institution.

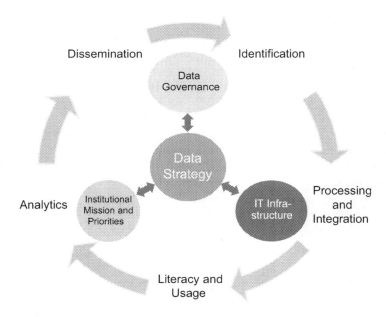

FIGURE 4.1 Data Strategy Environment

A data strategy thus exists in an interconnected environment that encompasses data governance, IT infrastructure, and the institutional mission and priorities to provide the core focus of all the data activities that occur within a college or university (Figure 4.1). A data strategy is the core of an institution's data life cycle. It draws from and guides IT infrastructure, data governance policies, and the institutional mission and priorities that drive the day-to-day data activities.

DATA STRATEGY PURPOSE

Fundamentally, a data strategy supports planning and management decisions in order to advance the mission of the institution. The value and importance of data are thereby emphasized within the institution, helping to promote a data culture that takes ownership of its data (Position Paper, Silicon Valley Data Science, 2015). A data strategy also establishes a clear roadmap for what to do and where to go next (Eckerson, 2011). This moves the institution away from a reactive and ad hoc approach informally described as "putting out fires" and moves it in a strategic direction that encompasses operational effectiveness and efficiency.

DATA STRATEGY CHARACTERISTICS

A data strategy includes an emphasis on data-based decision making; promotion of data efficiency through use and reuse considerations; and amplification of an organization's data resiliency, adaptability, and continuous improvement goals and practices (Levy, 2018). The strategy can be viewed in terms of defensive practices focusing on maintenance and protection or offensive practices spurring growth and innovation (DalleMule & Davenport, 2017). Ultimately, an institution must find a balance between these practices through careful consideration of priorities, needs, and limitations and the tradeoffs between data control and flexibility. Independent of context, a strategic plan of any kind has several key characteristics, described here with specific relevance to data (Hinton, 2012). These include but are not limited to the following:

Alignment with Institutional Goals

A data strategy maps technology to the mission and objectives of the institution. This eliminates and prevents redundancies and superfluous actions (Levy, 2018), thus ensuring that institutional goals are in alignment.

Adaptable to Change

The rapid change in technology necessitates a data strategy with a long-term ability to adjust while maintaining alignment with institutional goals (Position Paper,

Silicon Valley Data Science, 2015). In fact, a data strategy should be revisited regularly as part of a continuous improvement process yet must be malleable enough to allow for multi-year changes without having to start from scratch.

Flexible

Although similar to adaptability, the flexibility of a data strategy is the ability to stretch and bend in the face of short-term changes in data needs. This is in contrast to the more rigid nature of data control where data are regulated and uniform (DalleMule & Davenport, 2017). Nevertheless, a data strategy should be robust enough to last a few years before requiring significant changes.

Actionable

Along with the data mission of the institution, a data strategy needs to include clear goals and objectives with specific action items that integrate with other plans to form a comprehensive strategic direction (Position Paper, Silicon Valley Data Science, 2015).

Inclusive of Stakeholders

Who is implementing the strategy? Who is promoting the strategy? Who benefits from the strategy? Asking these types of questions will generate a list of data producers, owners, and consumers whose participation will be imperative to the adoption of a data strategy (Position Paper, Silicon Valley Data Science, 2015). This requires subsequent investigation and identification of these stakeholders' problems and needs which are essential to creating a relevant data strategy for the institution.

Value-Added

A data strategy provides more than just alignment and direction. It considers *how* the institution and its stakeholders benefit and not just *what* that benefit is. For example, leveraging data to optimize operational productivity allows the institution to respond to the needs of the college or university community as a whole, which may lead to positive shifts in the cultural climate or job satisfaction.

Sustainable

Ensuring that the strategy does not depend on volatile or unconfirmed resources is critical to its long-term sustainability. A poor understanding of institutional resources and long-term priorities can lead to the development of strategies that will require significant and potentially costly revisions down the road.

These characteristics allow for a data strategy to become a living plan, embraced and followed by the institution and its constituents. They are built into each of the key elements in a data strategy and provide vital guidance and focus.

COMMONALITIES OF A DATA STRATEGY AND AN IT PLAN

Every college and university has different goals and needs; consequently, a data strategy can vary from one institution to the next. However, there are several key data strategy elements that were described in detail in Chapter 2 – Key Elements of a Data Strategy – that every data strategy should include when integrating existing strategies, such as an IT plan, with the institution-wide data strategy. The following are eight brief highlights of the key elements as they relate to IT.

Data Goals and Objectives

What does the institution want to accomplish with its data in the long term? How does the institution see its data environment in the future? What data challenges confront the success of the institution's mission? The goals and objectives of a data strategy provide the direction for the institution's data functions. An IT plan can then align processes to support the institution's data mission.

Data Identification and Acquisition

This element begins with identification of data sources and types. It also defines common practices and conventions. How is data acquired and from what sources? Are there common practices for collecting data? Data typically falls into two categories: internal data generated from customer transactions (e.g., student applications, registrations and payments, disbursement of financial aid, grades) and external data created through third-party data or other external sources, such as governing bodies, state legislatures, federal regulators, or grantors of funds. Although an IT plan largely manages this element, the data strategy should accommodate a variety of data sources and plans into the institution.

Data Storage

How is data stored within the organization? Are there multiple ways data are stored? How is data secured from external infiltration? Data may be stored in silos based on department or business unit within a college or university. While IT planning handles most of the logistics involved (e.g., hardware, security), data storage should be part of the overall data strategy, mitigating redundancy between different departments.

Data Access

An institution's data are a valuable asset. There will always be people trying to gain access to them. Whether caused by a cybercriminal, a disgruntled employee, a competitor, or simply human error, data breaches can lead to compromise of institutional data. Data must be protected by carefully restricting access. Data should be prioritized at different levels to ensure sensitive information is protected and accessed only by authorized employees with legitimate reasons to view, obtain, or change it. Multiple state and federal statutes govern access to such data. Data access compliance is part of the data governance process and a function of IT planning.

Processing and Integration

Data integration involves using a combination of processes to merge data from disparate source systems. Data must be prepared, transformed, and/or corrected to make it into useful information. Data extraction and reporting are a result of the processing and integration phase. Once processed and transformed, data can be extracted and reports initiated.

Literacy and Usage

Data governance sets information policies, rules, and methods to ensure uniform usage, manipulation, and management of data. One reason for establishing a strong data governance process is to ensure that the rules and details of data are known and respected by all data constituents. Data governance establishes the framework for common definitions, data-naming standards, data rules, and decisions on how data are processed, manipulated, and shared. Governance also addresses access to data, how access is defined, and to whom access is granted. Both data strategy and IT plans must continuously collaborate with data governance to ensure consistent messaging.

Analytics

Once data practices are mature and reliability of data quality is assured, analytics can be leveraged to provide high-level insights into institutional progress and success. Appropriate software tools and effective communication are critical. Key performance indicators (KPIs) and data metrics can be developed to measure progress towards goals. Institution-specific indicators and outcomes for assessment and evaluation of progress towards goals can be derived from data sources.

DATA STRATEGY VERSUS IT PLANNING

Continuous Improvement

This step involves intentional and specific actions of evaluation and assessment that ensure continued efficiency and innovation.

The institutional data strategy unifies practices across the institution by providing consistency even at a granular level where data comes from a variety of sources and must be processed in a variety of ways. The following checklist incorporates the characteristics and elements of a data strategy into a quick assessment of data assets.

- Identify goals and objectives.
- Ensure alignment with data governance policies.
- Map data strategy objectives to IT infrastructure.
- Include key stakeholders.
- Determine reporting and analytics needs.
- Define KPIs and/or data metrics.
- Establish a clear roadmap.
- Apply continuous improvement evaluation.
- Document and share.

CORE ELEMENTS OF AN INFORMATION TECHNOLOGY PLAN

An IT plan is both operational and tactical. IT plans can be short or long term and allow for effective management of data for business transactions and operational flows to achieve organizational objectives. Business transactions or core services for many colleges and universities may include registering for classes, advising, class scheduling, financial aid disbursement, and payment of salaries to employees. An institution's IT plan may evolve from year to year based on new initiatives, technology, and regulations.

An IT plan defines projects and activities required to ensure successful implementation of policies, standards, and best practices as well as the pursuit of the institution's strategic plan. It provides personnel with a clear picture of their tasks and responsibilities and builds on existing infrastructure and capacity.

A successful IT planning life cycle (Figure 4.2) begins with a strategic roadmap and continues through stages of project planning, resource allocation, delivery of core services, and continuous improvement. Continuous improvement is needed to maintain quality and efficiency in the delivery of core services, and also for the institution to remain competitively resourced. IT plans leverage resources to support the mission of the institution by facilitating and streamlining day-to-day operations. IT plans help institutions manage their resources by specifying requirements for infrastructure hardware, software, people, security, access,

59

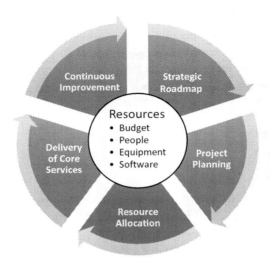

FIGURE 4.2 Information Technology Planning Cycle

and processes that deliver, protect, and enhance data and information assets through their various life cycles.

An IT plan aligns information resources with business requirements in part by establishing frameworks that emphasize information management. This emphasis defines projects and activities required to ensure successful implementation of standards, best practices, and policies required to ensure quality and consistency. An IT plan should describe the factors and business drivers that determine or influence the creation, storage, management, and use of information, including business needs, risk, and compliance with federal and state statutes.

An institutional IT plan should serve at least some of the functions listed here:

- Provide an information management methodology that defines projects and activities required to improve quality and efficiency.
- Provide project planning to support new initiatives driven by data strategy.
- Support, upgrade, and enhance business processes, software, and administrative systems.
- Evaluate and implement new technologies that improve operational efficiency.
- Provide a secure computing environment to ensure data privacy and integrity and to mitigate threats.
- Outline effective use of technology, resources, and systems.
- Provide the framework for data governance and access.

DATA STRATEGY VERSUS IT PLANNING

DIFFERENCES BETWEEN A DATA STRATEGY AND AN IT PLAN

A data strategy and an IT plan both strive for future results. A data strategy is institution-wide, has a long-term focus and is broad-based, so it is generally less detailed than an IT plan. It focuses on visions, values, and aspirations and is more mission-driven to adapt to disruptions or maintain a competitive nature.

An IT plan guides day-to-day operations that include organizational resources. It provides the foundation for the infrastructure needed to carry out a data strategy. An IT plan is typically short-term but can also be long term. IT plans are often specific to departments or units and involve basic communication, transactional data, and daily operations that take place on a college campus. Table 4.1 illustrates basic differences between a data strategy and IT Plan.

Although data strategies and IT plans are different, they are both dependent on data security measures. A data strategy focuses on intangible goals, such as long-term data security, reliability, and adaptability, while an IT plan focuses on more tangible resources, such as hardware, software, people, and training.

DATA SECURITY

Data security is the practice of protecting data from unauthorized use or access by using various hardware and software technologies. Securing data is often

Table 4.1 Comparison of Data Strategy and IT Plan

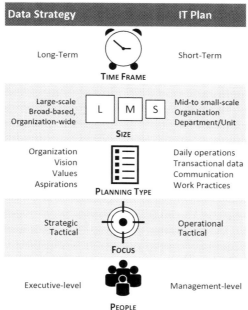

accomplished through the use of several tools, including antivirus software, encryption, firewalls, two-factor authentication, and software patches. Colleges and universities have been a target of cyberattacks for two primary reasons (Katz, 2005): first because of their vast amounts of data and computing power and second because of the open access they provide to constituents and to the public.

Data security is a crucial factor in IT planning and data strategy. It involves managing people, processes, and technology to ensure the physical and electronic security of an institution's data. A comprehensive security program is critical to protecting the individual privacy and confidentiality of education records. Data security is a key component of data governance and must be developed to account for the growing volume of unstructured data and network-connected devices, such as smartphones, on a campus that already provide vast amounts of data

Other risks that data security must mitigate include:

- Human error
  - Unintended disposal of data
  - Input errors
  - Mistaken processing of information

- Physical threats
  - Fire
  - Power outage
  - Theft
  - Malicious damage by employees

- External malicious activity
  - Malware
  - Breach of data from unknown source
  - Ransomware

- Unauthorized access to college resources
  - Databases
  - Internet, email systems
  - Processes for allowing access.

Unauthorized release of student data can have serious consequences for an institution, leading to financial losses incurred through fines, monetary judgments, or damage to reputation. College and university networks contain vast amounts of personally identifiable information (PII), making them prime targets for cybercriminals. Student data may contain social security numbers, medical information, confidential files, financial/credit card data, transcripts, disciplinary records, family information, and class schedules. Many of the data elements collected and maintained by a college or university are regulated by various laws or statutes.

Technological advances continue to outpace the creation of policies and laws that restrict or protect individual data and how it is collected and used by government entities, law enforcement, internet companies, hospitals, educational institutions, and others. Governments throughout the world have begun imposing new regulations on stored data and electronic communications. These regulations often define what information must be retained, for how long, and under what conditions. Many of the regulations are designed to ensure the privacy of the information contained in files, documents, and databases. Higher education organizations must comply with many regulations to protect sensitive information, including but not limited to the following:

- Family Educational Rights and Privacy Act (FERPA) – The Act gives students and parents certain protections regarding education records.
- Health Insurance Portability and Accountability Act of 1996 (HIPAA) – HIPAA is a set of standards set up to ensure the privacy of health information for patients.
- Payment Card Industry Data Security Standard (PCIDSS) – Applies to any organization that accepts credit card payments; covers a broad range of security requirements and processes.
- Gramm-Leach-Bliley Act (GLBA) – Applies to financial institutions and contains privacy and security provisions designed to protect consumer financial data. The law also addresses how institutions collect, store, and use financial records containing personally identifiable information.
- Fair and Accurate Credit Transaction Act of 2003 (FACTA) – Requires entities engaged in certain consumer financial transactions to be aware of the warning signs of identity theft and to take steps to respond to suspected incidents of identity theft. This applies to how institutions collect, store, and use student financial records.
- Federal Information Security Management Act of 2002 (FISMA) – Designed to protect the security of federal IT systems and data. The law applies to federal agencies, contractors, and affiliates, such as educational institutions that receive grants from a government entity. FISMA requires risk-based information security programs and independent review of those programs each year.
- State regulations – All states have enacted legislation requiring entities to notify individuals of security breaches involving personally identifiable information.

- European Union's General Data Protection Regulation (GDPR) — In effect since May 25, 2018, the regulation explicitly confers numerous rights to data subjects located in the European Union and requires organizations to put significant safeguards in place regarding the use and processing of the personal data of European Union residents.

Creating security frameworks that integrate the compliance requirements of the myriad regulations applicable to colleges and universities is a daunting task. The SANS Institute estimates that only 45 percent of higher education organizations have formal risk assessment and remediation policies in place; that figure drops to 31 percent for smaller institutions (those with fewer than 2,000 employees).

Data security is a component tied to both data strategy and IT planning. Within the context of a data strategy, data governance includes formal plans for leveraging and improving data security, as well as protecting and using data for competitive advantage. IT planning provides the infrastructure (hardware, software, training, and people) needed to implement data security practices within the institution. Data security is vital in both the short and the long term to ensure that day-to-day operations are secure, and that the financial interests of the college or university are protected.

DRAWBACKS OF A ONE-PLAN APPROACH

Often, a lack of resources (e.g., time, people, or funds) and/or a misunderstanding of data needs leads to the adoption or continued implementation of a one-plan approach to data planning and management. While planning is necessary, one plan may not be sufficient for the long-term data health and adaptability of an institution.

IT Plan Only

Many institutions already have an IT plan in place, which is only logical, given the long history of the IT realm and the accepted standards for databases, networking, hardware tech, and so forth. This is not without its drawbacks. As the Silicon Valley Data Science group states in their position paper, "It's tempting to charge off and begin deploying big data platforms and analytical capabilities, but without direct links to real problem solving, these investments can [flounder]" (Position Paper, Silicon Valley Data Science, 2015). Often an organization will purchase a tool without fully appreciating its integration and implementation within the context of data needs and challenges.

Additionally, an IT plan is often isolated from objectives at various levels of an institution despite providing guidelines related to the infrastructure and the capacity to store and manage data. Specialization and lack of general understanding can create a disconnect between the "IT guy" and the rest of the organization, leading to a culture that undervalues data. Consequently, focusing on an IT plan does not necessarily bring about the democratization of data at an institution, nor does it highlight the importance and value of data. In isolation, a data plan can seem like just another workplace hassle to deal with.

An IT plan tends to be reactive to the data needs of an institution. "We need data" or "We need to increase the capacity of our data warehouse" are examples of short-term, ad hoc demands that are met with in-kind solutions that do not drive innovation or decision making. For example, continued use of legacy technology and outdated processes can prove to be more costly than investing in new tools that are in line with an institutional data strategy.

Data Strategy Only

Adopting only a data strategy can be equally detrimental. A data strategy informs but also depends on effective IT and data governance plans. Without a solid IT infrastructure and an appropriate IT plan in place, a data strategy has no foundation on which to build to align with institutional goals. The resources needed to fully implement a well-intentioned data strategy may not be in place or even attainable.

An IT plan is necessary to preclude any assumptions about what is possible and provide the processes for coordination and management of resources needed for a successful data strategy. A data strategy alone provides the focus, objectives, and action steps for the long-term management of data to drive institutional planning and success. However, it does not spell out, for example, what security protocols to use, what servers are needed, what tools can be supported, or any specifics on IT software and hardware capabilities. This highlights two major considerations that a data strategy cannot manage: IT resources and best practices for software and hardware.

Benefits of a Two-Plan Approach

While data strategy focuses on the future (how to adapt and leverage competitiveness), IT planning is the process of creating and executing plans based on institutional resources and capacity. IT initiatives should align with strategic goals to create a transformative environment. The IT plan must support the overall data strategy. Without a data strategy, there will be no centralized vision or foundational structure for data initiatives within the organization. Each department will view data-related capabilities differently, which may lead to duplication of data and data systems throughout the organization, resulting in higher costs. Combining both plans creates an interworking blueprint that looks at multiple functions, levels, and locations and spans other natural or artificial divisions within a college or university. Using both plans supports strategic decision making by providing a comprehensive view of resources and commitments that ensures alignment of financial and capital resources with academic priorities.

Integration of data strategy with IT planning ensures that there is a system-wide understanding of both strategic and operational needs, capabilities, and priorities, as well as a system-wide alignment of vision and guidance on leveraging data as an asset. Different groups within the institution share a common view of data-related capabilities, thus reducing redundancy and confusion. Such alignment creates more consistency and often reduces operational costs and optimizes performance due to higher quality and reusability of data.

Data strategy also attempts to address some typical IT issues, such as the support of legacy technology that may hinder the adoption of innovative tools or business practices. Integrating data strategy and IT planning allows an institution to take stock of its current data environments and operations and establish a strategic direction for applying innovation with minimal disruption to ongoing business operations.

Figure 4.3 shows the data planning and management-strategy framework. The overall infrastructure created by combining the two types of plans is similar to the structure of a building. IT planning sets the foundation of the integrated set of plans. Building on the IT infrastructure, data governance provides another layer of the foundation for the overall data strategy and is included in both IT planning and data strategy. Data governance covers quality, security, access, stewardship, policies, compliance, and processes. The strong foundation from IT planning and data governance allows a stable environment to build the overall data strategy.

Institutions that take a holistic point of view in adopting a data strategy are well positioned to optimize their technology investments and lower their costs. By combining data strategy with IT planning, they treat data as an asset from which valuable insights can be derived. These insights can be used to overcome disruptions and also to gain a competitive advantage when they are integrated into day-to-day business operations.

Good governance of both data and technology is key to integrated data strategy and IT planning. Without a governance structure, data definitions are often ambiguous, and stakeholders squander time and resources trying to manage nonstandardized data. In the absence of an integrated approach, one group may undertake complex data analysis, including predictive modeling and business intelligence tools, yet be unable to share their results across the institution, which may cause stakeholders to duplicate work or miss opportunities.

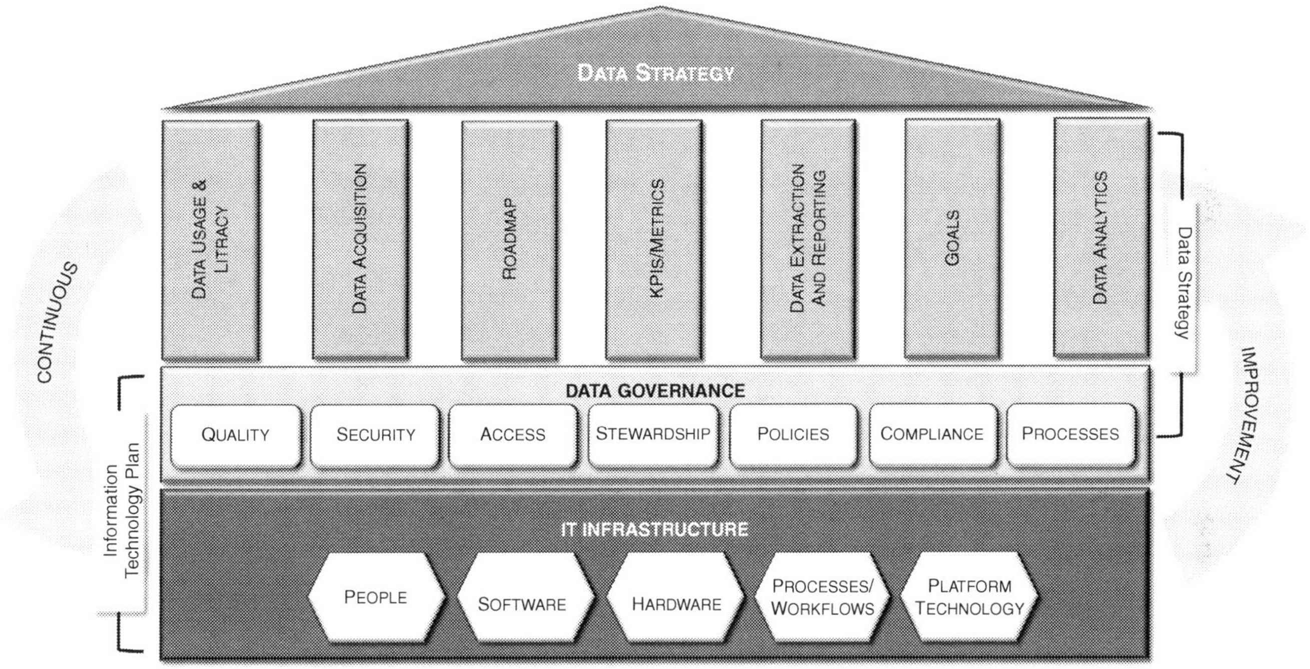

FIGURE 4.3 Data Planning and Management Strategy Framework

DISCUSSION QUESTIONS

1. How should an institution's administration communicate a data strategy so that the employees are engaged, involved, and empowered in its implementation?
2. How will staff understand that activities relating to the IT plan help support the institution's strategic objectives?
3. How will management and staff know if the two plans are working? How will they know if one plan is working and the other is not?
4. What differentiates a strategic framework from a planning framework in terms of conceptualization, development, and execution?
5. Strategies and plans have different audiences at different levels within a college or university. The college's president and executive team, faculty members, support staff, students, and alumni are all different audiences for data strategy and IT planning. Is there a common understanding of needs, priorities, and realization of benefits? Should information be explained using different language for each level? Should the language used to explain information vary by level?

REFERENCES

DalleMule, L. & Davenport, T. H. (2017). What's Your Data Strategy? [White Paper]. Retrieved June 21, 2018, from Harvard Business Review: https://hbr.org/2017/05/whats-your-data-strategy

Eckerson, W. (2011). Creating an Enterprise Data Strategy: Managing Data as a Corporate Asset [White Paper]. Retrieved June 21, 2018, from Higher Education Data & Information Improvement Programme: http://docs.media.bitpipe.com/io_10x/io_100166/item_417254/Creating%20an%20Enterprise%20Data%20Strategy_final.pdf

Hinton, K. E. (2012). A Practical Guide to Strategic Planning in Higher Education [White Paper]. Retrieved November 25, 2018, from Georgia Institute of Technology: http://campusservices.gatech.edu/sites/default/files/documents/assessment/a_practical_guide_to_strategic_planning_in_higher_education.pdf

Katz, F. (2005). The Effect of a University Information Security Survey on Instruction Methods in Information Security. DOI: 10.1145/1107622.1107633

Levy, E. (2018). The 5 Essential Components of a Data Strategy [White Paper]. Retrieved June 21, 2018, from SAS: www.sas.com/content/dam/SAS/en_us/doc/whitepaper1/5-essential-components-of-data-strategy-108109.pdf

Position Paper, Silicon Valley Data Science. (2015). Data Strategy: Developing Your Roadmap for Driving Business Value with Data [White Paper]. Retrieved June 21, 2018, from Silicon Valley Data Science: http://svds.com/wp-content/uploads/2015/10/DataStrategy.pdf

Part II
Implementation

Chapter 5

Leveraging Existing Information from Department Plans

Erin J. Holmes

INTRODUCTION

There are two models of institutional research (IR) practice: one described by Volkwein in his 2008 *Foundations and Evolution of Institutional Research* and the "New Vision" model outlined by Swing and Ross (Swing & Ross, 2016; Volkwein, 2008), as shown in Figure 5.1. In the Volkwein model, the relationship between IR and others in the campus community appears to be one way, with data emanating from institutional research to constituents. The Swing and Ross model, by contrast, appears to be one of data reciprocity, with data moving fluidly to and from IR in a matrix of relationships.

While only eight years separate the two models in Figure 5.1, the difference is striking and largely due to changes in technology. Data-discovery tools have become easier to use and ubiquitous (Swing & Ross, 2016). Despite IR's best efforts, access to these tools means that data have left the confines of the

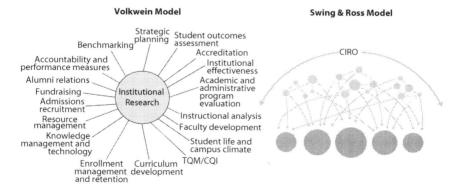

FIGURE 5.1 Two Models of Institutional Research

IR office and run into the halls of the academy. Often seen as threatening, this "democratization" of data should instead be viewed as an opportunity to leverage the skills and professional knowledge of many individuals at a given institution. As data moves into the hands of practitioners and knowledge is developed, IR practice will evolve into a coaching and orchestrating role (Swing & Ross, 2016). But as any good coach will say, a playbook is needed to guide the team. For an institution, this playbook is called a data strategy.

In the report *Institutional Research Capacity: Foundations of Federal Data Quality*, Randy Swing calls for the development of institutional data strategies throughout the postsecondary universe (Swing, 2016). In reality, as has been discussed throughout this book, there is a dearth of formal data strategies at the institutional level. Without formal strategies (or a playbook), the data environment can become chaotic. IR's role is often to tame this chaos. An enterprise data strategy provides a framework for this.

Dictionary.com defines strategy as "a plan, method, or series of maneuvers or stratagems for obtaining a specific goal or result (Dictionary.com. (Ed.), 2018)." Roger Martin offers a somewhat more expansive definition by stating that strategy is "the making of an integrated set of choices that collectively position the firm in its industry so as to create sustainable advantage relative to competition ..." (Martin, 2013, p. 2).

These definitions pertain to strategy overall, but how does one define a data strategy? In an article on the website Dataconomy, Lahanas states that an enterprise strategy is an integrated actionable strategy that is contextually relevant and changes with the organization (Lahanas, 2014). In support of the contextually relevant aspect of Lahanas's definition, DalleMule and Davenport describe a data strategy as being responsive to an organization's environment. In a high-compliance environment, organizations tend to adopt a defensive "Single Source of Truth" approach, whereas in highly competitive environments, they take an offensive posture with multiple versions of the truth (Dallemule & Davenport, 2017). It is no surprise, then, that since higher education operates in both high-compliance and competitive environments, its culture exhibits both types of strategic approaches.

The real pay-off in the development of a data strategy is in the creation of a process whereby a collection of facts (data) can be organized into information that supports knowledge and, in turn, wisdom. "Wisdom is integrated knowledge—information made super-useful by creating theory rooted in disciplined knowledge but crossing disciplinary barriers to weave into an integrated whole something more than the sum of the parts" (Cleveland, 1982, p. 34). It is wisdom, the combination of knowledge and experience, that can provide the foundation for action at an institution (Rao, 2018). The process of developing wisdom includes people interacting with data, creating information, and integrating that information with context into usable, actionable knowledge (Few, 2009). Because of this and the ubiquity of data-mining

LEVERAGING EXISTING INFORMATION

tools, the narrow role of IR as a data provider is no longer sufficient. The new model developed by Swing and Ross has IR both receiving information from its partners in the institution and providing it to them (Swing & Ross, 2016). This model revises the role of IR within the academy; because of IR's centrality within institutions of higher education, it must act as both a provider of information and a manager of knowledge.

This chapter will discuss ways to leverage information held throughout a college or university. While the chapter's title emphasizes information in department plans, the term "department plans" will be used expansively to include strategic plans, program reviews and assessments, accreditation documents, and reports developed within institutional silos. First, the chapter presents a knowledge creation model adapted for a higher education setting. It then suggests places to find existing information. Next, it discusses the application of traditional research methodology to the process of leveraging existing data and what to look for in existing information, the types of data used as well as the types that cannot be used, and how to enhance existing data. Finally, the chapter addresses how to bring all the data together in a cohesive whole.

KNOWLEDGE CREATION PROCESS IN A UNIVERSITY SETTING

There is a lot of literature about the process of creating knowledge. In a paper for IBM, Rao outlines the process using the DIKW (Data–Information–Knowledge–Wisdom) model, to which he applies principles of data science and machine learning (Rao, 2018). Figure 5.2, adapted from Rao (2018), expands this basic DIKW model for higher education.

FIGURE 5.2 Data–Information–Knowledge–Wisdom Model

73

The elements of wisdom are seen in the left-hand triangle. Essentially, the model traces the evolution of data to information, knowledge, and eventually wisdom, and also summarizes each of those concepts. The right-hand triangle applies the structures within higher education that work with the elements of wisdom. This adaptation thus incorporates the people and actions needed to create and leverage knowledge.

At the base of the model is data, defined as a collection of facts. In the higher education setting, data are compiled by IR for use by other actors on campus. The next level up is information, an organized collection of data used by IR and its partners to communicate an idea or a concept to a larger audience. Knowledge develops with the addition of context to information. Institutional partners add context for IR and context delivers wisdom to the decision maker. As Dalkir asserts "The only sustainable advance a firm has comes from what it collectively knows, how efficiently it uses what it knows, and how quickly it acquires and uses new knowledge" (Dalkir, 2005, p. 2). Wisdom arises when experience is combined with knowledge to generate concrete action.

WHERE TO LOOK FOR EXISTING INFORMATION

IR provides data across a given institution on nearly every facet of operations. Staff external to IR create the plans that transform data into information that then becomes knowledge. IR's task is to find the necessary strategic information; the following are places to look:

Report Inventories

The best place to find sources of information is often where IR has already provided data. A report inventory or audit tracks information sources. A report inventory is a basic tool in an IR office and an excellent source for leveraging existing data. The inventory provides information on reports, report purposes, and the people who requested the information. It is a map that identifies many of the partners, strategic plans, reviews, and documents for which data was provided. This identification allows the IR professional to pinpoint partners and leverage data from a variety of areas.

Partners

In an Educause *Viewpoint* article, Maas and Gower (2017) contend that there need to be partnerships between the chief business officer and the chief information officer in order for an institution to get the most out of its data. While this is true, the partnerships must extend further than this in order for an institution to gain maximum advantage from its data resources. Kirby and Floyd (2016) outline a number of offices with which IR needs to build strong relationships, including content experts (e.g., academic affairs, registrar, admissions) and external entities. Partners may be identified through the report inventory discussed above as well.

IR provides the data, while partners provide the context. Imagine, for example, a situation familiar to many IR professionals: being tasked by the leadership team with creating a presentation on enrollment trends. One approach is to produce a nicely formatted fact book; another is to regurgitate those same charts in a PowerPoint presentation that makes the data a bit more interesting to look at. However, both of these approaches fail to add context to the data, leaving the potential reasons behind the trends unknown. Partnering with a colleague in enrollment management makes it possible to give the data context. The enrollment management team might note that the steep decline in first-time freshman enrollments is due to the smaller high school graduating classes in the traditional service areas. Such context would turn data into information around which the leadership team could create an enrollment strategy.

College or Departmental Strategic Plans

Colleges and departments create strategic plans to guide their work and the futures of their programs. Often, they enlist the help of IR to develop the foundational elements of those plans, such as enrollment by major, student-to-faculty loads, faculty workload data, and salary information. Though IR has access to this data, the strategic plans place it in the context of the particular program or department. For example, IR may notice that total faculty salaries and the number of adjunct faculty both increased in a department during a particular period. The department would add context in the strategic plan by noting that several faculty members were out on sabbatical for that year and were replaced by adjunct faculty, driving up both the cost and the number of faculty.

Strategic plans can also be a source of creative data use that can change how IR provides data to the rest of the campus. A program may develop novel and valid ways to look at its majors or faculty. Broadly applied to the rest of the campus, this new view can inform practice on an institution-wide basis. For example, the chemistry department requests that IR examine a gateway course to see the percentage of non-chemistry majors who took the course to fulfill a program requirement. Chemistry might then use this metric to demonstrate the service the department provided to other programs across the university. By expanding this metric to other programs, IR could accomplish two things: demonstrate the interdependence of all programs at the institution as well as provide the chemistry department with benchmarks to compare the chemistry courses with those of the other courses at the institution.

Program Review or Assessment

Many colleges and universities require regular program reviews and annual program assessments. Both of these processes require a great deal of data from IR. They also provide a great deal of information to IR. As with data created for strategic plans, the IR professional should look for ways to extend the data requested (or required) for any program review or assessment to other programs. In addition, they should provide data not just for programs actively under review for a particular year but for all programs at the institution, thereby establishing a resource for answering program-related questions with a standardized set of data.

The IR professional should also be prepared to read program reviews and assessments for contextual information. As discussed earlier, IR provides data to programs and programs create context for the data. This context is a valuable source of institutional knowledge that IR is in a unique position to consume and digest.

Accreditation Documents

Accreditation documents an outline of an institution's past and a plan for its future. They contain a wealth of information that an IR professional can leverage. Again, IR often provides the data that forms the foundation of these documents, while the authors provide context, such as additional metrics to be created and monitored, weak areas that need further study, or programs and services that are particularly strong and merit more analysis to understand why.

For example, an IR office at a medium-sized university extended the use of an accreditation self-study by reading through the document, highlighting the areas of weakness outlined therein, and developing a research agenda around those weaknesses. Specifically, the school examined the retention and graduation rates of populations of interest and created descriptive reports in response. These reports have started broad conversations across campus surrounding student success.

WHAT TO LOOK FOR IN EXISTING INFORMATION: THE BASICS OF A GOOD RESEARCH METHODOLOGY

How does an institutional researcher determine if existing data are suitable for use in a research project? The first step is to recognize that IR is undertaking a research project and that the guidance for such projects already exists in the form of good research practice. The prevailing literature on research methods covers the use of information not directly collected by the researcher, what types of information are useful, and how to extend research to meet the needs of the project at hand.

The development of a research plan is essential to the successful use of existing data. The researcher needs to be clear on what is going to be researched, what existing information says about the research problem, and what data are available. A detailed research plan should include a problem statement or research question, a literature review, and hypotheses about potential outcomes.

Secondary Data Collection

It is helpful for IR practitioners to recognize that using data collected by others in their institution is fundamentally secondary data use and the accepted collection practices apply. First, what is secondary analysis? In Heaton's words, "Secondary analysis is a research strategy which makes use of pre-existing quantitative data or pre-existing qualitative research data for the purposes of investigating new questions or verifying previous studies" (Heaton, 2004, p. 16).

The purposes stated in this definition are key to IR practice. The investigation of a new question through secondary data collection is at the heart of this chapter on leveraging existing information. IR can determine the usefulness of any secondary data by understanding the purpose for the data collection and its relevance to answering the question currently under investigation.

Why should IR leverage data collected in other departments or use secondary data? First, it is faster and more efficient because the data are already available, allowing IR professionals to answer any questions that decision makers have more quickly. Data collection is expensive, so using existing information also saves the institution money. Finally, using existing data helps avoid the over-surveying of students as they are generally the object of the original research (Vartanian, 2011).

Disadvantages of using secondary data include a lack of control over both questions and quality. The research may not directly address a particular research question, or the data quality may be dubious. If IR is trying to investigate a current problem, the existing data may not be sufficient due to the timing of its collection. The use of secondary data may drive the types of questions asked because of its availability. Finally, secondary data may simply describe students, shedding no light on why they behave in certain ways (McCaston, 2005; Vartanian, 2011).

Vartanian suggests that researchers ask themselves a series of questions to help evaluate the appropriateness of secondary data use:

1 Is the focus population of the existing research appropriate to answer the question?
2 Can research connect the dependent variable to the data collected? For example, if looking at the impact of engagement on graduation,

can student graduation outcomes be tied to the National Survey of Student Engagement (NSSE) student responses?
3 Are the independent variables available in the research? Again, using the above NSSE example, if the researcher wants to study the impact of attendance at sports events on graduation outcomes, can that reasonably be done using the NSSE data?
4 Can the data be analyzed in such a way as to evaluate subgroups or populations of interest? Could the NSSE data be parsed to analyze women only or first-generation college students?
5 Is generalization to other groups important? If so, does the data lend itself to that?

(Vartanian, 2011)

Useful Types of Information

Not all information is suitable to leverage for use. There are no fixed rules about what is off limits, though good research practice and ethical conduct provide a solid framework for making a judgment regarding the appropriateness of information.

Some questions to ask before using data include:

- Are good research methods used in the collection of the data? Are the methods consistent with good research practice?
- How does the IR professional evaluate qualitative research?
- What are the ethical considerations in evaluating data to leverage in IR?

Are Good Research Methods Used in the Collection of the Data?

There are many criteria by which to ascertain whether data are collected in a manner consistent with good research. To demonstrate good research practices, let us consider a hypothetical scenario involving the use of NSSE at a small institution. Say the office of student life conducted the survey of first-year and senior students on its campus at what the institution considered to be a significant expense. As a result, the president wants to get the most possible use out of the results to promote student success.

The president thus asks IR to gauge satisfaction with institutional services and suggests that the IR office use the NSSE data to do so and to predict whether students would be retained or graduate successfully. This request makes two assumptions: engagement equals satisfaction, and satisfaction leads to student success. Could IR use a survey created to measure the concept of engagement to gauge satisfaction with institutional services? The first question that the IR office should ask is: does the concept of engagement equal satisfaction? The research concept of validity would point to "no" as the answer to this question. NSSE was created to measure a concept significantly different from satisfaction and thus should not be used to measure satisfaction. This is an example of a lack of face validity because engagement and satisfaction are two distinct concepts and cannot both be measured by NSSE.

IR returns to the president with a proposal to use the NSSE survey as it was meant to be used: to measure engagement, negating assumption one. This also shifts assumption two from satisfaction leading to student success, to engagement leading to student success: a different concept with the same outcome. Both face validity and construct validity (the "degree to which a measure relates to other variables ... within a system of theoretical relationships") tell the researchers that NSSE measures engagement (Babbie, 2017). It does so by capturing different engagement behaviors (such as number of times attending concerts or meeting with faculty) through survey questions.

How well NSSE can predict student retention or graduation in this scenario is the next question to address when examining whether to use NSSE. Do high levels of engagement relate to retention and graduation outcomes? This is criterion-related validity or predictive validity (Babbie, 2017). The first step in evaluating predictive validity would be to review the literature surrounding NSSE and its ability to predict the desired outcomes.

How Does the IR Professional Evaluate Qualitative Research?

IR professionals may be tempted to overlook qualitative data as a strategic data source. However, such data can be valuable in understanding the institutional context if collected through a rigorous research process. Qualitative research offers explanations for behavior. Hallmarks of good qualitative research include an articulated research design that describes the problem and research question, structured and standardized reporting, and analysis (Sullivan & Sargeant, 2011). The IR professional must evaluate qualitative research critically and know the difference between data and anecdote. It should always be remembered that the plural of anecdote is not data (Doyle, Mieder, & Shapiro, 2012)!

What Ethical Considerations are Involved in Evaluating Data to Leverage in IR?

There are a number of ethical considerations to take into account when deciding whether it is appropriate to use data collected for research by others within an institution. Many of these concerns are covered by the Institutional Review Board

(IRB) process within a college or university. Unfortunately, not all research goes through the IRB process, especially if it is being conducted for program assessment and evaluation. With this in mind, the institutional researcher should think critically with the following questions in mind. Was participation voluntary? Was anyone harmed in the production of this research, or could they be harmed by the results? Would the release of the information publicly cause harm to participants? Can anonymity and confidentiality be maintained if the research is used? Was deception used to collect the data or conduct the research project (Babbie, 2017)?

Many times, information produced by IR or other departments is confidential or proprietary, especially as it relates to enrollment management and enrollment projections. The institutional researcher should proceed with caution if the information could reveal strategic plans to competitors. The methods used to compile information that is confidential or proprietary, can be used, however. For example, enrollment management has developed a robust model to project enrollments for the upcoming term based on completed application counts and a variety of other factors. While the actual projections might be confidential, the model is not.

Generally, IR and others within a university design research projects carefully so as not to violate student privacy. Social research, by its very nature, attempts to uncover "truths" that can be applied to groups, not individuals (Babbie, 2017). Regardless, issues of student privacy must be paramount when leveraging data from other departments.

Enhancing Existing Information that Is Almost but Not Quite Useful and Discussing Limitations

Some of the limitations of using data collected by others were outlined above but warrant reconsideration here. Secondary data may have a different purpose than the research question and therefore may not be valid for the research at hand (Babbie, 2017). Another possible issue is incomplete information collection that does not include necessary variables to do follow-up research (McCaston, 2005). These limitations are not insurmountable. Some methods to get past them have already been discussed. Still, care should be taken to identify limitations and their impact on the outcome of the research, all of which should be carefully outlined in any presentation of the work.

As presented in the NSSE example above, one way to use data not quite suited to the purpose at hand is to reframe the research question. In that scenario, the IR office proposed that it use engagement (which NSSE measures) to predict student success. The original question revolved around satisfaction with services leading to student success. IR successfully reframed the question to measure the same outcome. Institutional researchers employ this method quite often while seeking clarity from those asking questions.

Replication of the research is another method of enhancing not quite useful data. This can help IR augment its knowledge of the original purpose of the secondary research and become more familiar with the data.

The final method is data triangulation, which is an attempt to relate different kinds of data to the same question or the application of different methods to the same question (Cox & Hassard, 2012). This method is particularly helpful when validating existing research. Does other available information support or refute research conclusions?

Creating Cohesion from All of the Parts

Pulling together all the information created by different units into a cohesive whole can be difficult but highly impactful. Despite its appearance at the end of this chapter, this challenge is better thought of early in the research process. The best way to create cohesion from all of the parts is to create a solid research design and proposal that guides the work for the project. This research design should include the traditional elements cited in the literature, most notably a clear guiding research question. What should be accomplished or understood when the research is complete? Does it have practical considerations or will the outcomes be actionable?

Second, a thorough literature review should be conducted so the researcher understands what has been written regarding both internal and external findings. This will provide insight into who internally may have similar questions or applicable research and where to look for data or information.

The research design should also identify who is to be studied. Will the subjects be students, faculty and staff, or alumni? The answer to this question will help guide the researcher to sources of data as well. The key variables in the study should be outlined carefully, which will help IR determine whether existing data will be sufficient for use in the study, if it will need to be supplemented with other data sources, or if new data should be collected. An important and often overlooked step in research design is a detailed description of how the data analysis will be conducted once the data sources are identified and data are collected. Without this planning, researchers may become overwhelmed by the amount of information collected and the project may be lost to "analysis paralysis."

> **DISCUSSION QUESTIONS**
>
> 1. Can you cite an example of when you extended a question that came from a program review request to other parts of your institution?
> 2. What are the advantages of secondary research and how can these benefit you in your professional work?

3. Why should an institutional researcher bother with creating a formal research design?
4. Can you cite some examples of reframing a research question?
5. How can a literature review be a valuable step in the process of leveraging information from other sources?.

REFERENCES

Babbie, E. (2017). *The Practice of Social Research* (14th ed.). Boston, MA: Cengage Learning.

Cleveland, H. (1982). Information as a resource. *The Futurist, 16*(6), 34–39.

Cox, J. W. & Hassard, J. (2012). Triangulation. In A. J. Mills, G. Durepos, & E. Wiebe (Eds.), *Encyclopeida of Case Study Research*. Thousand Oaks, CA: Sage Research Methods.

Dalkir, K. (2005). *Knowledge Management in Theory and Practice*. Burlington, MA: Elsevier Butterworth-Heinemann.

Dallemule, L. & Davenport, T. H. (2017). What's your data strategy? *Harvard Business Review*, 113–121.

Dictionary.com. (Ed.) (2018). Dictionary.com.

Doyle, C. C., Mieder, W., & Shapiro, F. R. (2012). *Dictionary of Modern Proverbs*. New Haven, CT and London: Yale University Press.

Few, S. (2009). *Now You See It: Simple Visualization Techniques for Quantitative Analysis*. Burlingame, CA: Analytics Press.

Heaton, J. (2004). What is secondary analysis? In *Reworking Qualitative Data*. London: SAGE. https://dx.doi.org/10.4135/9781849209878

Kirby, Y. K. & Floyd, N. (2016). Maximizing institutional research impact through building relationships and collaborating within the institution. *New Directions for Institutional Research, 205*(166), 47–59.

Lahanas, S. (2014). Why organizations need a data strategy. Retrieved from http://dataconomy.com/2014/11/why-organizations-need-a-data-strategy

Maas, B. & Gower, M. (2017). Why effective analytics requires partnerships. *EDUCAUSE Review* (May/June), 52–53.

Martin, R. L. (2013). Don't let strategy become planning. *Harvard Business Review*, 2018, (July 15, 2018), 2.

McCaston, M. K. (2005). Tips for collecting, reviewing, and analyzing secondary data, 1–9. https://cyfar.org/sites/default/files/McCaston,%202005.pdf

Rao, V. R. (2018). How data becomes knowledge, Part 1: From data to knowledge, 1–7. www.ibm.com/developerworks/library/ba-data-becomes-knowledge-1/index.html

Sullivan, G. M. & Sargeant, J. (2011). Qualities of qualitative research: Part I. *Journal of Graduate Medical Education*, *3*(4), 449–452.

Swing, R. L. (2016). Institutional research capacity: Foundations of federal data quality. Retrieved from https://files.eric.ed.gov/fulltext/ED592249.pdf

Swing, R. L. & Ross, L. E. (2016, March/April). A new vision for Institutional Research. *Change*.

Vartanian, T. P. (2011). Secondary data analysis. New York: Oxford University Press.

Volkwein, J. F. (2008). The foundations and evolution of institutional research. *New Directions for Higher Education*, *141*, 5–19.

Chapter 6

Self-Appraisal of a Data Strategy

Leah Ewing Ross, Jason R. Lewis, and Stephan C. Cooley

INTRODUCTION

This chapter opens with a simple question: So now what?

The first part of this volume provides valuable context for institution-wide conversations about data strategies. Specifically, Chapters 1 (The Value of Creating a Data Strategy) and 2 (Key Elements of a Data Strategy) open this section of the volume with a description of the key elements of data strategies and move us to the *how* of this work. Chapters 3 (Using Concepts from Strategic Planning) and 4 (Data Strategy versus Information Technology Planning) shed light on the *what* of data strategies, including their purposes and the ways they relate to other institution-wide efforts and structures.

Most colleges and universities do not need to start data strategy efforts from scratch because elements of data strategies likely already exist throughout the institution, either in informal pockets or in formal efforts, as Chapter 5 (Leveraging Existing Information from Department Plans) illuminates.

Perhaps more specific questions are needed to jump-start the self-appraisal of a data strategy: *Why* do we do this work, *what* do we seek to achieve, *who* is involved, and *how* is a self-appraisal accomplished?

THE WHY: KEEP THE GOAL IN MIND

Data strategies support decision making to accomplish institutional goals. However, if an institution has not defined its goals and clearly articulated its mission, a data strategy cannot exist. If an institution has not mapped out its destination (that is, what it seeks to achieve), knowledge about where the institution is right now simply does not matter because the information is floating without context or direction.

It is not sufficient for a college or university to have a plethora of available data and a well-organized data strategy that "looks good on paper." Data are virtually meaningless unless used as part of a strategy grounded in the institution's goals. Otherwise, the institution's progress toward achievement of its goals is elusive.

The transformation of data into information that supports decisions can help lead the institution to better outcomes. Just as landmarks guide a traveler, data and information serve as route markers or indicators of an institution's progress toward fulfillment of its mission. Self-appraisal adds value to a data strategy when it is firmly rooted in a framework of clearly defined institutional goals.

A data strategy is essential for an institution to achieve its student success goals. Although vitally important, a clearly articulated commitment to student success is not enough on its own, nor is the capability to identify struggling students. A college or university cannot address barriers to student progress without knowing *why* students are not succeeding. Thus, a data strategy should carry as much weight as a student success strategy. A data strategy is what fuels and undergirds all systems at the institution, ultimately supporting student success (Engle, 2016; Hosch, 2017).

"Doing Something" Isn't Enough

Most of us are familiar with the allure of "doing something" (versus doing nothing), especially when we feel compelled to solve a problem. In higher education, our motivation to do something often springs from our commitment to support students. Once a problem is identified, we explore it in the pursuit of greater understanding. However, exploration is not the same as doing something. We can use self-appraisal and other tools to gather copious amounts of information about what exists, but nothing will change unless we actually use that information to address the problem at hand.

This concept applies to the creation of data strategies, too. It is helpful to survey the landscape and identify elements of data strategies that already exist, but the mere act of doing so does not *create* a data strategy. Furthermore, the connections between data production, data use, and institutional goals are not automatic. Development, evaluation, and modification of a data strategy require intentionality at every level.

THE WHAT: DATA USE ACROSS THE INSTITUTION

Assessment of a data strategy—or the cataloging and evaluation of elements of a data strategy—is most useful when it captures all data production and use across the institution. We refer to the collective production and use of data and information as the institutional research (IR) function, or the data function, to differentiate it from the work of the IR office (Swing & Ross, 2016). The IR office produces and uses data, but it is not the *only* unit that does so. Mapping all data production and use is a large task, but worth the time and effort. At the most basic level, data work cannot be coordinated if it is not identified. In addition, the presence of a data function expands capacity, but only if it is acknowledged and encouraged. It is essential that no assumptions be made about data, such as what data exist, how they are collected and stored, and who uses them.

When the myriad places and ways that information is produced and used are well-documented, it creates the opportunity to ensure that appropriate sources are employed, contextual understanding is developed and applied, consistency is achieved, questions are addressed, redundancies are eliminated, and talent and expertise are shared. Furthermore, a robust data strategy provides space for innovation (Hosch, 2017). However, none of this can be achieved without a comprehensive strategy that encompasses all data and data sources and includes all data users and producers.

THE WHO: KEY STAKEHOLDERS

At some colleges and universities, data professionals are part of the senior leadership team, with the opportunity to contribute to institutional strategies and decisions to improve student success. Although not all data professionals serve in that coveted position, all have the opportunity—*and the responsibility*—to engage colleagues across the institution in data conversations. Data work is ever-evolving and should not be siloed; modeling inclusivity and collaboration is essential in pursuit of the institution's goals, even if senior leaders do not set the example. Each of us has a different scope of authority, but collaboration across the data function and among decision makers should happen at every level for all projects and initiatives, large and small.

Likewise, it is essential that the assessment of a data strategy extend beyond any one group of stakeholders or a specific tier of the institution's organizational structure. It must encompass a wide array of perspectives, including both producers and consumers of data and information.

In addition to mapping the institution's data function, the inclusion of a variety of stakeholders invites buy-in for a comprehensive data strategy and builds a resource network. The institution benefits when the community of data producers and data users is invested in developing and implementing a data strategy. It is important to acknowledge the human aspect of this effort, without which the work may be simply dusting off an evaluative tool. A successful self-appraisal is not just an assessment of the planning process that includes a survey of existing data and relevant processes. Rather, it is about ensuring the transmission of ideas within the data strategy so that they are implemented and resistance is mitigated.

In the realm of data strategies, higher education is unique because the legacies associated with leaders, faculty, staff, and the public create dynamics in which top-down authority and approaches applied in some other industries are not appropriate. Rather, process matters. Even the most sophisticated data strategy cannot be successful if it does not include input and garner buy-in from various stakeholders across all levels of the organization. The conversations that take place as part of this work can be difficult, whether the purpose is to identify sources of production and consumption of data, inquire about processes, or explore opportunities for change or improvement. Data professionals' passion for this work can result in experiences like the stages of grief when ideas and paradigms are challenged (McLaughlin, Brozovsky, & McLaughlin, 1998; Phillips & Horowitz, 2017). However, if acknowledged, this angst can be navigated, especially if it is handled in the spirit of discovery, with the goal of supporting student success.

THE HOW: A PROCESS

Just as a variety of approaches to plan and implement data strategies are needed by colleges and universities, different self-appraisal models are required, too. There is no definitive "right" way. However, key questions designed to facilitate dialogue about the purpose and underlying assumptions of the assessment process help ensure that it is contextualized, dynamic, and relevant. In addition, key indicators (Association for Institutional Research, 2019) ground an appraisal in the foundational components of a data function (Figures 6.1 and 6.2). Together, these key questions and key indicators keep the institution's goals and a focus on student success at the forefront.

Key Questions

Beginning a self-appraisal process of a data strategy can seem like a daunting and tedious task. The questions provided below are designed to help facilitate dialogue about the process in an effort to uncover any hidden assumptions and establish agreed upon goals. There are no right or wrong answers. Rather, the prompts are intended to help establish context and guide the appraisal from the start. This approach keeps the why, the what, the who,

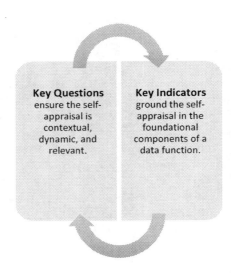

FIGURE 6.1 Self-Appraisal of a Data Strategy: Overview of the How

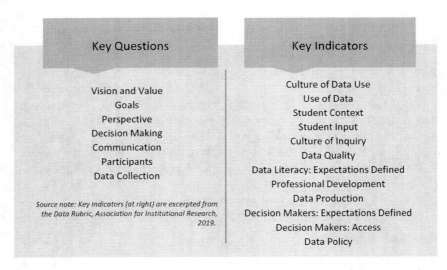

FIGURE 6.2 Self-Appraisal of a Data Strategy: Details of the How

and the how front and center so that they are not lost in the weeds of the appraisal itself. This clarity, in turn, promotes common understanding and transparency across participants and stakeholders, which are essential for a successful outcome.

Vision and Value

- What is the purpose of the self-appraisal?
- Why is it important?
- Who is the audience for this work?
- Does the process by which the self-appraisal is constructed and employed matter as much as the assessment itself?
- Is the self-appraisal a one-time snapshot or an iterative process?

Goals

DISCOVERY OF WHAT EXISTS

- What exists across the institution in terms of data, data access, data production, and data use, etc.?
- What are the gaps?
- Who is being served by the data strategy?

IDENTIFICATION OF WHAT COULD BE

- What components of a data strategy does the institution seek to incorporate, improve, or maintain?
- What components of a data strategy present challenges for the institution, and what are the potential solutions?
- How can the institution realize achievement in pursuit of the data strategy it desires?

Perspective

- What is the genesis of the self-appraisal? Did the assessment arise from a specific situation, event, or need?
- Will information about data production and consumption across the institution be gathered to support the institution's overall mission, values, and goals?
- Are there specific perspectives of focus to consider, such as commitment to equity, recognition of expanded sets of stakeholders, or preparation for accreditation processes?

Decision Making

- Who will be involved in making decisions based on the information gathered? That is, who—or what group—has the authority to change the data strategy based on the results of the assessment?
- What types of decisions will be made, and to what end?

Communication

- To whom will this work be described and communicated? By whom, how, and how often?
- How will messages be tailored for different audiences?
- Will the communication of findings be ongoing, or will they be reported once the appraisal is complete?

Participants

- Who will lead the self-appraisal process?
- Who needs to be represented in the process?
- Who are the key stakeholders?
- Who are the known producers and consumers of data and information?
- How will currently unknown producers and consumers of data and information be identified?

Data Collection

- What data and information are sought?
- How will participants' input be gathered?
- How will sources of information on data production and consumption be identified and gathered?

Key Indicators

Assessment of a data strategy cannot be "canned" or achieved with a generic template. If the self-appraisal is not contextual with a clear purpose shared among the participants and stakeholders, the information needed to determine whether a data strategy is meeting decision makers' and stakeholders' needs will be difficult to collect, inappropriate, and/or woefully incomplete. However, starting with a blank page is not helpful either. It is important to have a framework to guide the self-appraisal and to accomplish the goals identified through the key questions discussed in the previous section.

These indicators (Association for Institutional Research, 2019) ground exploration of and conversations about data strategy in the core elements of a data function. Each indicator can be evaluated to determine the extent to which it exists (e.g., a scale that ranges from "does not exist" to "fully realized"), captures "what is," provides focus on "what could be," and is relevant to the institution and topic at hand.

Culture of Data Use

Data must be viewed as valued assets for decision making and continuous improvement of the institution in order for a robust data culture to exist. *Self-appraisal of a data strategy should determine the extent to which it supports a culture of data use.*

To what extent does the data strategy support institution-wide data use to:

- Meet requirements?
- Address stakeholders' expectations?
- Engage in continuous improvement?

Use of Data

As noted at the beginning of this chapter, student success is a critical goal an institution should seek to achieve through its data strategy. Yet data have no value if they are not used, and the mere use of data does not ensure *appropriate* or *valuable* use. *Self-appraisal of a data strategy should determine the extent to which it supports data use to explore student success.*

To what extent does the data strategy support institution-wide data use to:

- Identify student performance gaps?
- Address student performance gaps?
- Continuously evaluate student performance gaps?

Student Context

Placing student success at the forefront of data work requires nuanced attention to the student experience by subgroup, such as first generation, age, race/ethnicity, major/credential program, etc. *Self-appraisal of a data strategy should determine the extent to which it supports expectations of employees to contextualize the student experience.*

To what extent does the data strategy support contextualization of the student experience:

- By staff?
- By units and programs?
- By faculty?
- By administrators?
- Across the institution?

Student Input

Support of student success requires the inclusion of student input. Despite the fact that we are surrounded by ever-growing sources of data, efforts must be made to ensure that the student perspective is included. *Self-appraisal of a data strategy should determine the extent to which it supports integration of student feedback in decision making across the institution.*

To what extent is feedback from students:

- Gathered? and by whom?
- Accessible? and by whom?
- Used? and by whom?

Culture of Inquiry

Inquiry is at the heart of higher education, through academic scholarship and the institution's exploration of itself. Cultivation of a culture of inquiry requires intentional design. *Self-appraisal of a data strategy should determine the extent to which it supports the institution's use of data for self-examination to address myriad lines of inquiry.*

To what extent does the institution use data to address:

- Internal lines of inquiry?
- External lines of inquiry?
- Stakeholders' needs?

Data Quality

If data are not reliable, they are not used, or their use leads to erroneous conclusions. *Self-appraisal of a data strategy should determine the extent to which it supports and enhances data quality.*

To what extent does the institution facilitate:

- Collection and use of reliable data?
- Awareness of the value of reliable data?
- Maintenance of reliable data?

Data Literacy: Expectations Defined

An institution cannot achieve a data-informed decision culture without a commitment to the data literacy of both data producers and data consumers (Lewis & Ross, 2017). *Self-appraisal of a data strategy should determine the extent to which it supports expectations for data literacy.*

To what extent are data literacy expectations:

- Defined?
- Established across the institution?
- Contextualized by unit, program, or role?
- Communicated?

Professional Development

Expectations for data literacy are not realistic or achievable if they are not paired with relevant support. *Self-appraisal of a data strategy should determine the extent to which it supports professional development for data literacy.*

To what extent does professional development align with expectations:

- Of staff?
- Of units and programs?
- Of faculty?
- Of administrators?
- Across the institution?

Data Production

It is likely that, every day, the sources and amount of data available increase within the institution. Yet if not managed and organized, data production may not provide the information needed to achieve the institution's goals. *Self-appraisal of a data strategy should determine the extent to which it supports coordination of data production.*

To what extent is data production coordinated:

- Beyond mandatory reporting and accreditation?
- Beyond the IR office?
- Between units?
- Across the institution?

Decision Makers: Expectations Defined

A data-informed decision culture cannot be realized if expectations for decision makers' use of data are not clearly defined. *Self-appraisal of a data strategy should determine the extent to which it supports expectations for data use in decision making.*

To what extent are expectations for data use in decision making defined:

- For staff?
- For units and programs?
- For faculty?
- For administrators?
- Across the institution?

Decision Makers: Access

Clarity about data culture, data use, data literacy, and expectations is all for naught if decision makers do not have access to the data they need to inform their work. *Self-appraisal of a data strategy should determine the extent to which it supports the availability of data for decision making.*

To what extent is relevant data access provided for decision making:

- By staff?
- By units and programs?
- By faculty?
- By administrators?
- Across the institution?

Data Policy

Without effective data policy, formal or informal, the previous indicators cannot be explored. *Self-appraisal of a data strategy should determine the extent to which it supports data policy.*

To what extent does data policy:

- Govern and protect the institution's data?
- Ensure individuals' privacy?
- Reflect stakeholders' input?
- Require collaboration across the institution?
- Align with the institution's goals?

THE SO WHAT: USING RESULTS

The information produced during a self-appraisal has value only if it is used to create or revise a data strategy. Often, the greatest challenges are organizing and analyzing the information gathered. If the institution's goals serve as the focal point, and the key questions and indicators described above serve as the framework, a clear roadmap will emerge, allowing the data strategy to be a pathway rather than a collection of disparate initiatives. At every stage, the "so what" must be probed to avoid doing something for the sake of doing it, overcomplicating things by falling prey to a "more is more" perspective, and obscuring the work, thereby thwarting transparency.

It is highly unlikely that a thorough self-appraisal will reveal that everything is operating smoothly, and that the institution's data strategy is perfect. The institution's context is not static. Ever-changing dynamics among policies, practices, and people result in the frequent need to make changes, large or small, to support the successful pursuit of the institution's goals. Sometimes findings challenge people's assumptions, egos, and ways of doing and being. Yet such difficulties can be navigated by ensuring that the perspectives of all data producers and data users are represented in the self-appraisal and that results are communicated in an approachable, inclusive manner. There is much to gain when a collaborative style is employed.

DISCUSSION QUESTIONS

This chapter is organized around questions for self-appraisal. As such, discussion questions may feel like more of the same. However, these questions may be used to help prepare for the work outlined in the chapter, or to frame high-level discussion about self-appraisal of a data strategy among stakeholders (e.g., an IR/data office retreat, a graduate course, or to initiate a collaborative endeavor shared by several units).

1. What is known about the data function at this institution?
2. How can we embark on exploration of yet-unknown sources of data production across the institution?
3. Does a data strategy exist at the institution? If yes, is it formal or informal?
4. If we engage in self-appraisal of our data strategy, what is the goal?
5. What do the key questions shared in this chapter reflect about our institutional data culture overall, and our data strategy (or lack thereof) in particular?
6. What do the key indicators shared in this chapter reflect about our institutional data culture overall, and our data strategy (or lack thereof) in particular?
7. Are data policies at this institution formal or informal? If informal, is formalization of relevant policies a priority?

REFERENCES

Association for Institutional Research. (2019). *Data rubric*. Tallahassee, FL: Author.

Engle, J. (2016). *Answering the call: Institutions and states lead the way toward better measures of postsecondary performance*. Seattle, WA: Bill & Melinda Gates Foundation. Retrieved from http://postsecondary.gatesfoundation.org/wp-content/uploads/2016/02/AnsweringtheCall.pdf

Hosch, B. J. (2017). *Beyond data governance to data strategy* [Conference presentation: Association for Institutional Research Forum, May 2017]. Retrieved from www.stonybrook.edu/commcms/irpe/reports/_presentations/DataStrategy_Hosch_2017_05_31.pdf

Lewis, J. R., & Ross, L. E. (2017). *Building a data-informed decision culture* [Course paper: A Holistic Approach to Institutional Research]. Tallahassee, FL: Association for Institutional Research.

McLaughlin, G. W., Brozovsky, P. V., & McLaughlin, J. S. (1998). Changing perspectives on student retention: A role for institutional research. *Research in Higher Education*, 39(1), 1–17.

Phillips, B. C. & Horowitz, J. E. (2017). *Creating a data-informed culture in community colleges*. Cambridge, MA: Harvard Education Press.

Swing, R. L. & Ross, L. E. (2016). A new vision for institutional research. *Change*, March/April 2016, 6-13. Retrieved from www.airweb.org/Resources/IRStudies/Pages/A-New-Vision-for-Institutional-Research.aspx

Chapter 7
Anticipating Challenges and Offering Possible Solutions

Shannon Rose LaCount and Michael J. Weisman

INTRODUCTION

Say the term *data strategy* to anyone, and it will likely conjure visions of numbers, spreadsheets, and rows of ones and zeros. It will summon up images of graphs, charts, and tables but no sense of the human effort required to create them. Have a discussion with someone actively working on a data strategy for their campus, though, and their list of challenges will likely include both technical and non-technical elements, such as relationship building, personnel, and accountability.

BACKWARD DESIGN FOR A DATA STRATEGY

When developing a data strategy, it is wise to start with the end in mind and consider backward design, a common concept in education related conversations. Introduced by Wiggins and McTighe (2005), it provides a framework for designing a curriculum by focusing on desired outcomes and then creating learning activities, materials, and assessments to achieve them. A similar framework can be used for a data strategy and may serve to identify and work through challenges—or ideally avoid them altogether.

The parallels between curriculum and data strategy design illustrate the utility of starting with the end in mind. When designing a curriculum, the intended result is that learners learn. In data strategy design, the intended result is to give consumers or users the information they need to do their jobs, make decisions, and ultimately improve their programs. Challenges as well as solutions associated with this work have both technical and human elements, both of which will be addressed in this chapter along with change management and engagement of stakeholders.

CHALLENGES AND SOLUTIONS

One universally applicable solution to most challenges is having clearly defined terminology, intentions, actions, and anticipated results. In teaching and learning design, outcomes answer the question "Why?" (*Why am I giving this assignment? Why am I taking this class?*). In data strategy design, outcomes formalize or define the purpose of a data strategy and provide answers to such questions as, *What do we need to know about your campus? What trends can we uncover? What stories are useful and to whom? In what form(s) is the data best provided?* It is through backward design concepts that we better understand challenges and solutions that remedy the root problems.

There is a common tendency to jump to technology solutions rather than really understanding the challenges or root causes behind the challenges. (Kinney and Wang elaborate on the differences between information technology (IT) planning and a data strategy in Chapter 4.) If transformational leaders are not involved in the active design decisions throughout the process, the software is not going to meet the needs of day-to-day end users. This section includes discussion of eight challenges and solutions (Figure 7.1)

Identifying Audiences and the Data They Need

Flash back to just a mere 20 years ago and creating, structuring, and managing data collection was a big challenge. Now, the opposite is the case—institutions have too much data, much of which goes unused. In fact, most campuses are swimming in data. The current challenge is processing data into information or meaningful forms to support action. Which data are deemed necessary and how

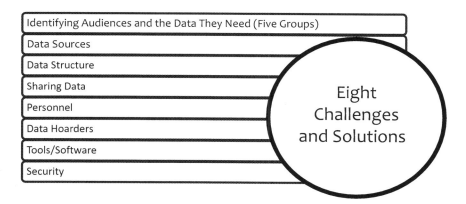

FIGURE 7.1 Eight Challenges and Solutions

they will be disseminated and used depends on the role and perspective of the end users, who include administrators, faculty, student affairs professionals, institutional research (IR) specialists, IT analysts, and students and their families. In some cases, users are either consumers or creators of data; in others, they are both.

Administrators as an Audience

Administrators' campus-wide perspective allows them to view data from across the college or university to inform decisions about budget, resource allocation, and strategic actions. Given the vast amount of information that administrators consume, it is less important to focus on data entry, creation, or input (although these are universally important considerations) than on the accessibility and format of data output. The best solution is to give administrators access to configured dashboards and executive summaries that target specific details. Comparing results across departments or over time to reveal trends are useful benchmarks for administrators to determine program effectiveness, relevance, and associated resource allocations. Old or incomplete data can lead to frustration and possibly even wrong decisions (described further in Chapter 8 on Presidents' and Provosts' Perspectives).

Faculty as an Audience

Individual faculty members are best served by teaching and learning data collected through tools such as student evaluations of instruction and learning analytics, which can inform decisions about how they manage and conduct their courses. Faculty are both creators and consumers of data. At a minimum, they produce grades that can be used as measures of course success. In a more robust (and likely meaningful) teaching and learning process, faculty will assess and record the degree to which students meet learning outcomes. This can take the form of a score on an assignment, rubric, exam, or measure of their choice.

More detail in the data means more value to the faculty member and the institution. As mentioned earlier, collecting learning data aren't typically the challenge. Gradebooks, learning management systems (LMSs), and assessment management systems (AMSs) provide ample opportunity to record scores and store them electronically. The challenge is connecting, processing, and returning that data in a meaningful format.

To meet the data needs of faculty, consider easy-to-adopt and simple solutions. Provide tools and opportunities for data *collection* to occur as part of their teaching process (e.g., an assessment rubric that calculates a score or grade, returns results and comments to students, produces learning analytics, and connects to institutional assessment efforts). For data *consumption*, ensure easy access to teaching and learning data in a meaningful format. Routinely provide professional development and support—in multiple formats—for processes and tools involved in your data strategy, no matter how simple they may seem.

Faculty groups involved in programmatic decisions about curriculum or assessment will benefit from aggregate views of learning data, enrollment trends, course success, and student achievement data. In this role, faculty are consumers of data and should benefit from the same considerations that apply to administrators. However, customized permissions that reveal only data relevant and appropriate to the situation may also be necessary.

Student Affairs as an Audience

Student affairs professionals provide a wide array of programs and services. They face the challenge of demonstrating how programs and services have an impact on student success. Thus, student affairs professionals need views of data that inform the management of their programs and services to ensure the most positive impact possible on students' well-being and success.

Student affairs administrators will benefit from the same data and formats as academic administrators, providing a strong argument for using a connected system with customizable permissions to avoid "siloing" data or duplication of effort. Further, student affairs professionals can be both consumers and creators of data. Collecting student affairs-related data can be tedious, but it doesn't have to be. It is also important to assess for whom the student affairs data might be useful.

Student affairs programs and services are designed to involve and engage students and support their learning and personal development. Knowing which students are participating in these opportunities can reveal trends in how and when they do so and, better yet, can help gauge the impact of student affairs programming. The data created in these scenarios is clearly useful for resource and budget decisions, but less commonly acknowledged is the value of such data to faculty who are looking to connect their course content to experiences outside the classroom and to students themselves.

Data Professionals as an Audience

Institutional research and information technology professionals are often most concerned with how accurate data are, how easy they are to manage and disseminate when requested, and how data will be used and interpreted when shared. They are most often consumers of data and creators of customized views of data in the form of reports and dashboards. These groups require convenient access to a centralized database, data that doesn't require cleanup, options for export and reporting for mandated requirements such as Integrated Postsecondary Education Data (IPEDS), and tools that help limit redundant or repeated requests. Periodic program reviews, discipline or programmatic specific accreditation reports, and regional accreditation reports often request similar information regarding enrollment trends, learning outcomes results, as well as program or institutional effectiveness. Use of systematic and centralized tools can maximize the utility of data processes for various reporting interests.

Students and Their Families as an Audience

Students and their families are the most commonly overlooked audience in data strategy. Prospective students and their families want to see data that communicates the types of experiences an institution offers and how well it promotes learning, employment, and success. Now more than ever before, data can predict student success, communicate alerts before it's too late, and offer encouragements supporting a growth mindset.

Current students need information to help them make decisions about course selection(s), program and event participation, to best navigate through higher education processes for timely degree attainment, and successful pursuit of employment or admission into a subsequent degree program.

While students will likely not be involved in direct data entry, their actions can generate a sea of useful data. Pre-enrollment, non-cognitive, learning, and behavioral data can help predict where and how a student may need support. A data strategy that connects consumers of student data can help with early alert programs, support systems, and targeted interventions that can be used prescriptively and proactively to keep groups as well as individual students on a path to success.

Data Sources

Data are everywhere on campus, but their quality and usefulness can vary. After establishing which data are necessary and how they will be used, it is time to determine where data currently exists or will be coming from and what state or format they are in. To determine if needed data already exists, start with the data creators. Identify what aspects of their daily routines and activities generate information, determine if the processes used to gather that information are effective and efficient, compare the formats of the resulting data (Word document vs. Excel, codes, etc.), and then confirm that the data are available to those who need it.

If data does not already exist, determine how it can most easily be generated and by whom. Data must exist in order to be used, but collecting them can be tedious. If there is no clear purpose to the task, it can be done halfheartedly, leading to errors or gaps in data and ultimately to misinformation. This may also lead to gaps in data. Using outcomes as an example, if leadership does not provide a compelling purpose for reporting towards outcomes, inconsistent collection of data and perhaps an incomplete portrait of learning may result.

The following are a few tips for data collection:

- Provide clear definitions.
- Consider the perspective of the people collecting or generating the data.
- Create a simple path to collection and/or acquire the appropriate tools.
- Communicate the destination(s) for the data (i.e., how it will be used).
- Share results with the stakeholders doing the work to collect the data.

Where data exists matters, and it is important to be conscious of the number of sources involved. Neither centralization nor dissemination is inherently good or bad, and both are required for an effective data strategy. For example, single data sources are often used for enrollment data and demographic data, which are usually kept in an enterprise resources planning (ERP), customer relationship management (CRM), or student information system (SIS).

These locations are often considered the system of record and serve as the final and official source. This can be good because the data are up to date, consistently and reliably coded, and all in one place, making them easy to locate. On the other hand, access can be an issue if there is a curmudgeonly gatekeeper (a concept addressed later in the chapter), a long process for requesting and receiving data, or no way to connect to related data.

Data from multiple sources has its own set of considerations. Many data types—among them learning data, faculty research activity, and student services usage—will logically come from multiple sources in a variety of formats. Therefore, multiple contributors need to understand the data strategy. To avoid problems associated with multiple sources of data, be sure to provide the professional development and training necessary for contributors to successfully use collection tools and adequately understand the data itself. Sharing results, reports, or short summaries of how the data are used in other areas can help convey the bigger picture to those who may be frustrated by what they perceive as busy work.

To illustrate our points on multiple data sources, consider Scenario 1 in Figure 7.2.

A campus offers a guest-speaker series targeted at first-year students but open to all students and the community. The series was designed to address the campus's strategic theme of "Promoting Entrepreneurship" and fulfill a requirement for students seeking a leadership certificate (a co-curricular pathway). It is also

> recommended as an extra-credit opportunity for a course in the business management department.
>
> To ensure effectiveness and inform planning for the following year, an assessment of the series includes usage data (attendance), satisfaction (follow-up survey), and learning data (rubric assessment of an optional reflection essay).
>
> Data collection takes place as follows. When attendees arrive, they are asked to record their name and email address on a sign-in sheet. Students working toward their leadership certificate have one week to submit a reflection of their experience to the director of the leadership program, who distributes their essays to one of five possible reviewers with access to the rubric and, for those students enrolled in the business course, to the relevant faculty member. A survey containing five questions about the speaker and ten about the series is sent to all attendees. All results are shared with the coordinator of the series, the director of the leadership program, and the faculty member teaching the business course. Results from the five speaker-specific questions are shared with the speaker.

FIGURE 7.2 Scenario 1

Information is collected and housed in multiple formats and locations. Attendance is collected once, on paper. It is easy to locate but difficult to use. Somehow, it needs to be connected to demographic data, to determine the number of attendees belonging to the target audience (first-year students), and enrollment data, to determine the number of attendees enrolled in the business class. The attendee list is also necessary to administer the follow-up survey.

Reflection essay rubric results are generated by six different evaluators —five for the leadership certificate and one for the business course. The results will allow the director and faculty member to determine which students are eligible for credit and will also inform the strategic planning committee evaluating data associated with the "Promoting Entrepreneurship" campus theme.

Yet another consideration is how to gather survey data. With a single collection method such as an online survey, results can be connected to demographic and enrollment information, filtered, and disseminated to stakeholders. If survey data are collected in multiple formats, results are more difficult to manage. While a variety of options are possible, considering scenarios like this one can be useful in developing an effective data strategy.

Data Structure

One possible pitfall when designing a data strategy is choosing to collect data because it is easy, not because it is useful. Another is letting juicy data pass you by when it could be used to make great improvements. Meaningful and useful data come in multiple forms.

The most commonly reported are enrollment numbers, demographic points, graduation rates, and other kinds of quantitative data. This structured data, made up of clearly defined data types, is specifically formatted and stored in an organized way, making it easily searchable for later processing and analysis. The words "easy to count, store, and manipulate" are music to the ears, but structured data only provides part of the picture.

Fifty-three to 80 percent of data available for analysis is *unstructured data* (Chakraborty & Pagolu, 2014), such as audio, video, and text data. Unstructured data are everywhere and incredibly useful but do not follow the typical row-and-column structures of databases and are therefore rarely captured and less often used (DalleMule & Davenport, 2017). Both kinds of data, structured and unstructured, come with their own challenges. For structured data, consider developing a clear and well-communicated naming convention, which will save hours of work and limit the chance of error because data won't have to be manipulated, changed, collated, or mapped.

Creating a naming framework should be a priority from the very beginning of developing a data strategy. This will ensure that data creators have input on the coding structure and terminology and help avoid confusion when there are multiple sources of data. There are also situations where the coding structure will be dictated by mandates or standards used by required databases. For example, the National Center for Education Statistics (NCES) developed the Classification of Instructional Programs (CIP) to support accurate tracking and reporting of fields of study and program completion. Using CIP codes for courses and programs will facilitate the task of anyone who needs to use them for mandated reporting.

As mentioned earlier, unstructured data does not follow the conventions of a traditional database, making it more difficult to access and analyze. However, that neither negates its importance nor prohibits its use. Text analytics is a powerful method for providing structure and gleaning value from unstructured data. A quick Google search will reveal endless options for methods and coding languages to use for text analysis. In the end, including unstructured data in a strategy is worthwhile but requires dedicated personnel with the capabilities and tools to conduct the analysis.

Sharing Data

A good way to avoid frustration and misinformation in a data strategy is to treat higher education institutions like the complex ecosystems they are. Systems thinking in a data strategy context means that one must consider the consequences of one's actions on the experiences of others within the system—not a common practice given how siloed higher education can be. A well-executed data governance process will not only consider naming conventions, permissions, access, and collection practices, but will also clearly communicate data destinations (the places where and reasons for which data will be used) and emphasize that changes to codes or other adjustments made in one office or program will have consequences for others on campus. Consider the two scenarios in Figures 7.3 and 7.4 to illustrate these points.

In 1980, a campus admissions office began collecting an emergency contact phone number for every admitted student on a paper form filled out during enrollment. Those emergency contact numbers were entered into the student information system (SIS) by a person whose primary job was data entry. Two years ago, the admissions office decided to streamline the process and move the form online.

They took the opportunity to shorten the form and eliminate "all demographic data collection," as this information already appeared on the students' applications. Once the form had been moved online, the person in charge of data entry was given a new role and no longer accessed the SIS. Because the person who implemented the change considered the emergency number "demographic information," it was removed from the form.

There was no cross-reference check with the source of the demographic information—the application form—to confirm that an emergency contact number was included. Because the data entry role had been eliminated, no one realized that the emergency contact field in the SIS was blank. The admissions office was not aware that the advising staff's only source for emergency contact numbers was the paper form in a student's file. One day, an advisor was looking for an emergency contact number and, unable to find the form, asked for access to the phone number in the SIS, only to find the field blank. This is a problem.

FIGURE 7.3 Scenario 2

ANTICIPATING CHALLENGES, POSSIBLE SOLUTIONS

> A university's SIS contains a "first-generation status" field where the official code FGEN is used to identify first-generation students. Students' first-generation status is self-reported data collected from surveys conducted through six different programs on campus. Each program uses the data to inform its work and is asked to provide the data for entry into the SIS. Because each program has its own survey-collection method, each also has its own method for sharing the data. One program emails the names to the SIS administrator, four provide a spreadsheet with student identifiers (id: 12345 codes: Trad or FirstGen), and the last enters the information directly into the SIS with the code "1stgen."
>
> University administrators apply for a grant to fund a First-Generation Student Center and need to report the percentage of first-generation students and current first- to second-year retention rates. To get the percentage, a report is run for #of students FGEN. To get the retention rate, a query asking for "first-gen status field=true." This is a problem.

FIGURE 7.4 Scenario 3

The problem in Scenario 2 could have been avoided by discussing the key change with the person initially responsible for data entry, identifying all the places on campus where the emergency contact number was being used, and ensuring a path to the database through other means.

The university in Scenario 3 did have a defined naming convention but still had a problem because that convention wasn't clearly and routinely communicated, and the data creators did not know how it would ultimately be used. The following are a few steps that campuses can take to support a data ecosystem:

- Make naming conventions easily accessible to data creators.
- Ensure resources and training are included in onboarding for new employees.
- Communicate sources of data in reports and executive summaries.
- Schedule regular checks of databases.

Personnel

What factors help mobilize personnel to pursue data-driven strategies? Possible catalysts include a changing of the guard within the ranks of senior leadership to support strategic goals, pressure from the board of directors to provide transparent and timely access to data for oversight and governance, and accreditation reports highlighting the need for enhanced data strategies. Sudden changes in enrollment of new students or retention and graduation rates can also impact data strategies. Finally, purchasing and implementing new technologies may influence personnel requirements.

Once the alarm bell goes off, the institution should assign responsibility for defining and executing a data strategy to either select personnel or a committee. Given the fiscal constraints at most institutions, addressing a data strategy is typically not anyone's sole focus. The additional responsibility can impact the quality of work as well as the timing of completion. Considering data-driven practices are a relatively new concept in academia, existing personnel may not have relevant experience, requiring them to learn as they cross this new frontier.

Creation of a sound data strategy requires input from the institution's data stakeholders. Those responsible for developing a plan are tasked with identifying, quantifying, and measuring pain points; for example, what resources are being wasted through use of inefficient data? This can be a challenging exercise since some constituents may struggle with communicating their data issues.

Use of technology is often perceived as a solution to data issues, but by no means will it solve personnel matters. While technology may speed up the transaction of data, it typically does not eliminate the need for people to input, analyze, or react to the data. In many instances, implementation of new technology has identified poorly defined processes, gaps in data oversight or the need for either one-time or, more likely, continuous training of personnel.

Data Hoarders

As previously noted, there are benefits to having a centralized location for data. An SIS, ERP, or CRM is intended to be a single database that stores key information in an organized way. Data can be extracted in a standard format and repurposed in all relevant areas on campus. Unfortunately, centralization can also enable data hoarding.

Data hoarders can be present in every area within the college or university. Unintentional data hoarding can take place when only one person on campus can access the database and write the code to extract the information. Limiting access to a database full of sensitive information makes sense, but if the one authorized person can't keep up with data requests, the database will be of little utility. Solutions to this type of data hoarding include having enough staff to meet demand and/or having tools that make it easier to respond to requests. Data visualization and dashboarding tools allow those with access to the main database to create live, refreshable views so that end users have the most up-to-date data at their fingertips, with no need to submit a request.

Data hoarding can also happen in systems. Branch campuses are often at the mercy of the system offices that manage databases containing necessary information. Policies and practices designed for systemic efficiency may not meet the needs of individual campuses. Campuses should know of or investigate any potential system policies or limitations on data and consider them when designing their data strategy.

There are also, sadly, intentional data hoarders—well-meaning people with a strong sense of responsibility who are skeptical about how data are going to be used and believe access to them should be limited. The solutions to this challenge are paying careful attention to permissions, clearly defining reasonable use of data, and identifying who should have access so there are no arguments when requests are made.

Tools/Software

Software solutions are a necessity for any data strategy, and they can range from simple data collection tools to massive databases. It is also important to remember that software is a tool for accomplishing a goal or objective; it is not a replacement for work. Software audits are common practice. Intended to evaluate and assess which technologies are currently available on campus, they can lead to a decision to add new programs or make a switch from old, outdated software. Depending on one's point of view, this can be a challenge or an opportunity.

While software doesn't eliminate human effort, it should enhance it. It can create connections and be both a vessel for collection and a medium for sharing results. When vetting software options, campuses must consider the components necessary to achieve the goals of the data strategy, the technical skills and abilities of data creators and consumers, the training and support options offered by the software vendors, and data security. Campuses have a lot of options to choose from. Rather than figuring out what they can do with a platform, they can now decide which platforms have what they need to accomplish their goals.

The software as service (SAS) model reduces the cost of creating and maintaining tools and opens up access to a team of developers dedicated to making those tools better; however, it also limits control and customization options. In the end, any chosen software should help the institution accomplish the goals of its data strategy, put access and permissions in the control of the campus, support the work of data creators, and help answer the questions of the data consumers. It should also be efficient, less manual, more sophisticated than current programs, and appropriate for the scale of the campus.

Security

Meaningful use of data means using meaningful data. Unfortunately, that can require personally identifiable information (PII), health information protected and regulated by the Health Insurance Portability and Accountability Act (HIPAA), and student education records and information protected by the Family Educational Rights and Privacy Act (FERPA). Institutions need this data to accommodate reporting requirements, make meaningful changes to curricula, provide health services, and support students and staff, but making sure it is available to the right people in a safe and appropriate manner carries risk. The key to data security is eliminating as much risk as possible without eliminating appropriate access.

The greatest risk to data security on campus and in any setting is what Jason Ehlert, Vice President of IT Operations at Campus Labs, calls *the human factor*. "Take the people out of the mix and our networks will be secure" (Ehlert, 2019). Campuses can have thousands of people logging on to their systems for millions of reasons.

Each person may have various levels of exposure to technology, limited knowledge of what is considered secure or not, sensitivities to what is considered personal or private information, a range of comfort with sharing personal or private information, and a lack of awareness of what needs to be protected. The solution to the human factor is education; there is no way around it. Data security practices and risk-awareness training should be incorporated into all onboarding, professional development, and annual review activities.

The second security consideration is software. More and more software solutions are moving to the cloud. This can eliminate the cost of hardware and maintenance of servers on campus, but it puts the onus of data security in the hands of a third party. Campuses can ensure that their chosen software meets security standards by using the EDUCAUSE-developed Higher Education Cloud Vendor Assessment Tool (HECVAT). The HECVAT is intended to "ensure the cloud services are appropriately assessed for managing the risks to the confidentiality, integrity and availability of sensitive institutional information and the PII of constituents" (EDUCAUSE, 2019, p. 1).

CHANGE MANAGEMENT AND ENGAGEMENT

Implementing any new strategy means accepting change. A change in leadership may be the catalyst for, or the result of, a data strategy. Institutions will need to encourage a *data-sharing attitude* in current campus members accustomed to a siloed system and look for signs of such an attitude in new hires. Programs and activities will need to be put in place to foster data and technology skills and data literacy.

Academia is inherently skeptical, and talk of data collection, storage, and use can conjure fears of Big Brother. Clear, honest, and frequent communication can go a long way toward quelling those fears. Encourage scholarly debate, an optimistic form of disagreement, rather than its more negative cousin, conflict, by providing the following ways for stakeholders to engage with the data strategy:

- Create paths for input in strategy development.
- Communicate how and why data strategy decisions are made.
- Model good use of data.
- Share examples of how data can improve and enhance the campus.
- Tell stories using data.
- Offer opportunities to work with data so campus members can understand how they are generated and can see future applications.
- Demonstrate how assumptions can be proved, disproved, or changed if the right data are available.
- Explain the consequences of making a change to the way data are collected (or not).
- Show the end vision. Get people excited about the goal, and then talk to them about what it will take to get there.
- Encourage accountability and reward good data use.

Strategies for Effectively Engaging Campus Leaders

When faced with data strategy challenges, a common knee-jerk reaction for senior leadership is to identify and purchase new technology. The logic being that big data and technology require software not the expertise of people. However, in pursuit of implementing the technology, the data challenges are often not resolved, but rather brought into greater focus. In order to reset expectations of the "magic" technology offers, senior leadership need to appreciate that people work alongside technology.

Connected Data Ecosystem

It is also important to identify types of data fluency personnel need to have in order to leverage technology to enable them to do their jobs more effectively. Some of this is born from the presumption that technology is intuiting your need and proactively providing it to you. For instance, assuming a beautifully presented data dashboard is going to give you explicit direction on how to address a strategic initiative opposed to serving as a window into data you decipher and draw conclusions from.

At Campus Labs, when we engage a college or university to address a connected data ecosystem, we recommend leadership be involved from the very beginning of the process. We do this via a data governance team. We broadly define data governance to include data stewardship, data infrastructure, and data fluency (Jackson, 2019). Data stewardship is about empowering transformational leaders—personnel that have autonomy and power to make decisions on behalf of the institution and are empowered to use data to inform day-to-day and long-term activities.

Getting Data People and Non-Data People Involved

It is important to have a space where IT personnel and front-line data users such as faculty and staff are talking together as the data infrastructure is being developed. If one or the other leads the decision about how to build this ecosystem, frustration and failure is likely to follow. It can be challenging for those that don't have an IT background and support to help set up and automate the flow of data and connection of data into tools. In those cases, functional leaders aren't going to feel like they have the right data or the information they need in order to use those data in the way that we're trying to promote continuous improvement. Data fluency is building a culture of using data. How do I interpret a dashboard? How do I make sense of this information? How do I actually use information to make changes on campus?

The best way to meet the needs of various stakeholders is to give them a seat at the table during the design phase. In a traditional governance model, a few people—typically directors or leaders—represent key departments, and it is incumbent upon those individuals to be comprehensive in their recommendations and actions. But a new model may be necessary—one where the people who benefit directly from an effective data strategy are contributing to the conversation.

CONCLUSION

A data strategy should be a resource, not a burden. At a minimum, welcoming a variety of voices helps to ensure that they've been heard and allows for the creation of a comprehensive list of needs. Inclusive data strategies can be a resource and an inspiration.

There are various methods for inclusion. Campuses can form groups focused on data strategy that are either ad hoc, existing only during the planning phase, or permanent and advisory as the strategy is launched and requires adjustments. Some institutions develop an academic intelligence vision and designate a leader who concentrates on the campus as a whole.

Others are driven by mandates or ongoing review, so they start in offices of assessment or educational effectiveness and expand involvement from there. Similarly, enrollment and business considerations may drive the strategy. Regardless of the catalyst, it is important to consider the attitudes or mindsets of the individual members in addition to their perspectives. The group should be willing to make connections and collaborate across independent departments, bring data together, share it appropriately, and understand where the campus is versus where it wants to be.

"Not everything that can be counted counts." While the origin of this saying is debatable, the meaning holds true. Improvement and innovation are well served by meaningful information. This is best achieved through a process where all stakeholders have an opportunity to be heard, which informs the institutional data strategy.

DISCUSSION QUESTIONS

1. Which challenge resonates with you the most at your institution? What suggestions and strategies that the author provided do you think would be most useful? Why? Why not?
2. Who are the audiences for a data strategy at your institutions? Select two audiences and discuss at least one of the eight challenges included in this chapter. Include potential solutions, drawing on suggestions from this chapter.
3. Which challenges already exist at your institution? Which had you not considered when creating a data strategy?
4. This chapter discussed data hoarders. Since they can add considerable new content to, as well as distract from, a data strategy, what approaches would you take to find the data hoarders and involve them in the process?
5. Change is inevitable. Discuss change management strategies that would be applicable for your campus to minimize chaos in the data ecosystem.

REFERENCES

Chakraborty, G. & Pagolu, M. K. (2014). Analysis of unstructured data: Applications of text analytics and sentiment mining. Retrieved from https://support.sas.com/resources/papers/proceedings14/1288-2014.pdf

DalleMule, L. & Davenport, T. H. (2017). What's your data strategy? *Harvard Business Review*. May–June 2017. Retrieved from https://hbr.org/2017/05/whats-your-data-strategy

Dweck, C. S. (2006). *Mindset: The new psychology of success*. New York: Random House.

EDUCAUSE. (2019). Higher education cloud vendor assessment tool. Retrieved from https://library.educause.edu/resources/2016/10/higher-education-cloud-vendor-assessment-tool

Ehlert, J. (2019). Personal communication.

Jackson, M. (2019, September 5). Data governance and continuous improvement: Lessons learned for best practice [Blog post]. Retrieved from http://www.campusintelligence.com/2019/04/24/data-governance-and-continuous-improvement-lessons-learned-for-best-practice/

Wiggins, G. & McTighe, J. (2005). *Understanding by design* (2nd ed.). Alexandria, VA: Association for Supervision and Curriculum Development.

Part III
Perspectives

Chapter 8

Presidents' and Provosts' Perspectives

Ivan L. Harrell, II

INTRODUCTION

Presidents and provosts have some of the most rewarding and challenging roles in colleges and universities. In a time when higher education institutions are being challenged to provide excellent education to students, with increased accountability, decreased funding, and increased needs to provide students with more than academic resources to succeed, the ability to lead becomes even more difficult (Gagliardi & Turk, 2017). In addition, there is growing scrutiny of the value of higher education, particularly as it relates to preparing students to secure jobs that pay living wages. To ensure that their institutions remain successful and relevant in this climate, it is critical that presidents and provosts engage in data-informed decision making. This chapter focuses on meeting these competing challenges while creating a data strategy that advances the institutional mission.

DESCRIPTION OF THE PRESIDENT AND PROVOST POSITIONS

The role of the president is to lead the college or university to achieve its mission. In fulfilling this role, the president serves as the chief executive officer and typically reports to a board of trustees. The president is charged with providing overall leadership and vision for the institution. In particular, the president is responsible for ensuring that the college or university is meeting the needs of its constituents (students, faculty, staff, alumni, community members, trustees) while remaining fiscally solvent. The president is also responsible for providing direct oversight of other executive officers, which may include the chief academic officer, chief financial officer, and chief student affairs officer.

Due to the varying structures of colleges and universities, the exact title of the president and other executive officers may vary. The provost typically serves as the second in command of the institution as well as its chief academic officer, providing direct oversight and leadership for the academic program. Provosts often have additional duties, such as directly supervising other major areas of the institution. In many cases, they are responsible for running its day-to-day operations.

DIFFICULT COMPONENTS OF THE POSITIONS

The roles of president and provost are both rewarding, but they also present many challenges. Figure 8.1 highlights three of these, which are further described below. A data strategy could turn these challenges into opportunities and strengths.

1. Equitable Outcomes: While colleges and universities must transform themselves to provide more equitable outcomes for students, faculty, and staff, institutional change is often met with resistance and can take time. Distribution of resources that translates to equitable outcomes does not happen overnight. And even with a strategic plan, such efforts are tough. Including equitable outcomes in a data strategy could accelerate the process.
2. More Key Stakeholders: There have been calls for greater accountability and transparency to provide better outcomes for students while dealing with decreased local, state, and national support, and thus increased reliance on revenue generated by student tuition and fees (Gagliardi & Turk, 2017). This part is not new. However, in recent years, more people have taken seats at the institutional table, claiming their status as key stakeholders. This more crowded table has increased the complexity of navigating the diverse needs

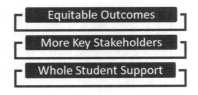

FIGURE 8.1 Difficult Components of the President and Provost Positions

of internal and external constituents, including students, faculty, staff, alumni, community members, elected officials, and trustees (The Aspen Institute, 2017). As a result, presidents and provosts have found themselves strategically developing a campus culture that embraces, and appropriately acts upon, work to promote equity, diversity, and inclusion (Soares, Gagliardi, & Nellum, 2017). Given that the data interests and needs of key stakeholders vary, a data strategy to manage their multiple and sometimes competing data requests is essential.

3. Whole Student Support: Support systems that address the welfare of the "whole student," such as food pantries, housing assistance for homeless or near-homeless students, and emergency funding (Soares, Gagliardi, Wilkinson, & Hughes, 2018) are no longer just "nice to have" or limited to institutions that primarily serve low-socioeconomic students. Even students with a solid education and financial plan can experience setbacks (family illness, loss of a job, divorce, etc.) that deprive them of their personal supports, leading to education failures and/or delays. Data analyses that focus exclusively on campus activities (e.g., academic and co-curricular)—in other words, those that only use data found in a student information system—represent woefully missed opportunities to promote student success, alumni involvement, and contributions to the community. Thus, data strategies need to go beyond college experience data and reach out to better understand the "whole student."

RELIANCE ON DATA

Given their senior leadership roles, it is crucial that presidents and provosts be equipped with as much timely information as possible to allow them to make the best decisions. The need to not only obtain good data but also to turn that data into information for decision making is becoming more important, particularly with the increased accountability of colleges and universities (Gagliardi & Turk, 2017). While senior leaders want all information to be as accurate as possible, perfection is not worth the cost of getting critical information after a decision has been made.

Student Demographic and Characteristic Shifts

As the student population of many colleges and universities becomes more diverse, presidents and provosts rely heavily on data to more clearly understand the unique needs of students and to respond accordingly. Student data, both quantitative and qualitative, should inform and influence every aspect of institutional operations (Gagliardi & Turk, 2017). Demographic data are particularly helpful, allowing the institution to fully understand the profile of the student body and how that profile may have changed, or may change in the future.

As one participant in the American Council on Education Presidents' Roundtable said, "institutions that don't focus on these demographic shifts will suffer the consequences" (Soares, Gagliardi, Wilkinson, & Hughes, 2018, p. 2). Data regarding student academic performance, such as course completion, term-to-term retention, graduation, and completion rates, is critical as it informs changes that may need to be made to academic programs and admissions policies, as well as the development of support programs that meet the individual needs of each student. It is also extremely important that presidents and provosts always receive this data in a disaggregated fashion, to enhance their understanding of a diverse student body.

Since the enrollment of many colleges and universities fluctuates over time, presidents and provosts must be able to rely on strong enrollment data (Soares, Gagliardi, & Nellum, 2017). These leaders need to understand the size and characteristics of the student body, how enrollment as a whole has changed over time, how enrollment may change in the future, and which student populations seem to be changing at rates that differ from those observed for the student body overall. This information is vital for institutions that depend heavily on student tuition and fee revenue to function. Thus, data strategies that focus on identifying shifts in addition to reporting data updates will position senior leaders to more appropriately respond to students' needs while managing a fiscally responsible budget.

Enrollment and Faculty Hires

Committing to hiring the appropriate number of full-time faculty to teach students is one important decision with significant financial implications. Having too few faculty means that students are not able to enroll in the courses they need; having too many could mean that expenses exceed revenue, inevitably leading to reductions in other areas. Thus, accurate enrollment forecasts are critical.

Unfortunately, the enrollment predictions for the upcoming fall are typically out of sync with faculty hiring processes, which take place many months earlier. It is therefore clear to senior leaders that enrollment estimates serve as the basis for making decisions. Regular enrollment updates that impact decision making need to come sooner rather than later (e.g., the week before classes begin).

Finances

Ensuring the financial stability of colleges and universities is a major responsibility of presidents and provosts. There is a need to understand how the finances are distributed throughout the institution and how much it costs to run academic and support programs, as well as individual divisions and departments (Soares, Steele, & Wayt, 2016). It is imperative that presidents and provosts have accurate financial data when making critical decisions that impact certain parts of the institution or the institution as a whole. As state and federal funding for many colleges and universities continues to decrease, the reliance on financial data increases.

This data should inform all major decisions, such as those associated with starting and ending academic programs, expanding the institution's physical footprint, increasing and decreasing the number of faculty and staff, or improving the institution's technology infrastructure (Gagliardi & Turk, 2017). Data strategies that integrate student data analyses with financial analyses are extremely beneficial, sparing leadership teams from having to marry together multiple unlike reports from multiple departments; improvements can be gained here.

CURRENT CHALLENGES IN ACCESSING AND USING DATA

Although presidents and provosts must use data to inform decision making, there can be certain challenges in accessing and using data as an individual and as an institution. This next section covers four of these; suggestions for addressing each challenge in a data strategy are included.

Data Infrastructure

One of the major challenges is having the ability as an institution to develop and sustain an effective data infrastructure (Gagliardi & Turk, 2017). The institution must not only employ the right number of data staff, but these staff must also be properly trained to collect, analyze, and disseminate data. An effective data infrastructure is also dependent on having data technology and software that can effectively meet the data demands of the institution (Soares, Gagliardi, & Nellum, 2017). The challenge for many colleges and universities in developing such an infrastructure is typically not a lack of understanding of its necessity but rather a lack of resources to create and sustain it.

Creating a Forward-Moving Data Culture

Even in colleges and universities that have an effective data infrastructure, presidents and provosts may struggle to establish a forward-moving institutional culture in which data are trusted, understood, and used broadly. A key takeaway from the American College President Study 2017 is that "Cultivating positive attitudes toward the collection and use of data enables a culture on campus that elevates informed decision making at all levels across the campus" (Soares, Gagliardi, Wilkinson, & Hughes, 2018, p. 6).

One major challenge with this is that many faculty and staff have not been properly trained to use the data that institutional research (IR) offices may be providing. This typically results in a reluctance to use data to effect change within the institution. In some cases, institutions have not dedicated sufficient time and resources to educating the campus community about what data are available, how they were collected, how they were analyzed, and how they can be used. A consequent lack of understanding causes some people to question the validity of the data, particularly when those data challenge their own notions about the work that they are responsible for completing (Gagliardi & Turk, 2017).

Senior Leaders Modeling the Data Culture

Creating a data-informed culture is a major responsibility of the president and, even more so, of the provost. It begins with developing the executive team. Sometimes presidents inherit a team that has not embraced the need for a data-informed culture; other times, they may have to hire someone who has the expertise to lead a major area of the college or university but lacks strong data experience. In these instances, there must be an intentional effort to create and maintain an executive team that not only understands the importance of using data but can also communicate that importance to their team and serve as good role models for the entire institution (Soares, Gagliardi, Wilkinson, & Hughes, 2018).

On-Demand Accessibility to Data

From time to time, for all college and university faculty and staff—including presidents and provosts—a challenge they face is accessibility to needed data. Although presidents and provosts have the power and authority to request data at any time, in certain situations they may need critical data immediately. If colleges and universities have not provided easy access to the data, these leaders may not have the information they need to make well-considered decisions quickly. Worse yet, they may be pushed to make decisions based on anecdotal or outdated data. All data strategies should thus include plans for senior leaders to have ready access to key data reports in straightforward formats.

PRESIDENTS' AND PROVOSTS' PERSPECTIVES

WHAT WE REALLY WANT DATA PEOPLE TO UNDERSTAND

As mentioned, the role of a president or a provost is important and complicated. Quality data must always be available to inform the many decisions that these leaders have to make on a daily basis (Soares, Gagliardi, & Nellum, 2017). Therefore, it is vitally important that institutional researchers and other data experts get to know and clearly understand what the specific data needs of these leaders are. This section addresses five key points that most presidents and provosts want their data experts to know in order to be successful in their roles (Figure 8.2). Each key point is described before this section concludes with other words of wisdom for data professionals.

Transform Data into Information

Institutional researchers and other data team members should understand that although presidents and provosts need data, their real need is for data that have been transformed into an actionable format. Results of data analysis must be presented in a way that is concise and tells a clear story. Additionally, the answer to the president's or provost's original request should be easily found in the deliverable.

Inclusion of an executive summary is also important. It allows senior leadership to quickly understand the data being presented and move on to the most important task—making actionable decisions based on that data. In short, transforming data into information is paramount. While detailed information may be needed on rare occasions, presidents and provosts are generally not interested in receiving a large data set that they are then left to analyze themselves; they prefer to rely on their qualified, capable data experts for analysis.

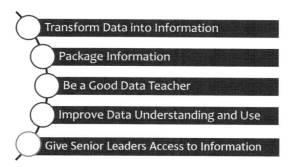

FIGURE 8.2 Key Points that Presidents and Provosts Want Data Experts to Understand

Package Information

Using data that are consistent, correct, and from the same source should be among the core principles for creating analyses and reports. One of the most frustrating things for a president or provost is to receive data that seem to contradict earlier data presented by the same office/department. It may be necessary and appropriate for multiple departments to divide and conquer a request from senior leadership. Presidents and provosts expect that department heads will work together to accomplish tasks; we do not expect one person to know everything.

Suggested Best Practice

For example, a request regarding enrollment forecasts could involve admissions (potential new students), IR (data analysis), and finance (impact on budget). It is preferable that one department head take the lead to organize the data request and make sure all aspects of it are covered. Once the separate units have completed their work, the lead organizer should look at the information as a complete package, reviewing it both for consistency, to eliminate confusing or contradictory information across reports, and accuracy, to correct human error.

The lead should then write an executive summary that synthesizes all of the individual reports. The executive summary should be shared with other department contributors for their feedback and sign-off. The final materials should be submitted to the president as attachments to a single email stating that all contributors have reviewed and signed off on the executive summary. All contributors should be copied on the message.

This approach sends a clear signal to the president that the materials have been through a rigorous and collaborative review and thus merit the time it will take to read and digest the information. Even if questions remain about the analysis and data limitations, leadership will appreciate the thoughtful, collaborative effort and will gain trust not only in the data but also in the data experts presenting it. This approach is much preferred to the alternative, where leadership receives data from multiple sources and must put the puzzle pieces together.

Be a Good Data Teacher

Data experts and institutional researchers must also have (or develop) the ability to explain—not only to the president and provost but also to the institution at large—the data they are presenting. Sometimes data are presented to the campus community in a way that assumes that everyone has some understanding of data terminology and data analysis techniques, and the ability to clearly comprehend what is being shown (Gagliardi & Turk, 2017; Soares, Steele, & Wayt, 2016).

In most cases this assumption is not true, as many faculty and staff have received little to no relevant training. Therefore, it is very important for data professionals to be able to understand who their audience is, quickly assess their data skill sets, and use that information to present the data in a comprehensible way. In many respects, a good data professional must also be a good teacher.

Improve Data Understanding and Use

In addition to being able to function as teachers, data professionals also have to address the disconnect between their view of adequate data accessibility and that of the campus community (Gagliardi & Turk, 2017). This type of disconnect becomes evident at many institutions when people do not use data resources (dashboards, reports, etc.) that are produced by data offices. There are frustrations on the part of both the data makers and the data users.

In many instances, the data team has made data available on websites, intranets, and other places, but members of the campus community still feel as though the data are not accessible because they do not know how to use the data sources. In short, availability is not the same thing as accessibility. Once again, it is incumbent upon the data professional to teach the campus community not only how to access the data but how to understand and use them as well.

Give Senior Leaders Access to Information

Presidents and provosts have to be able to access data, sometimes very quickly. These leaders are often in situations where there is an immediate need to share information with constituents. Data professionals are encouraged to meet with senior leadership to understand their individual and group data needs, as well as how they prefer to access data. At a minimum, presidents and provosts should have dashboards that outline the data most important to them (The Aspen Institute, 2017). They should be able to access these dashboards on and off campus, as well as on mobile devices. Data professionals are also encouraged to meet with new presidents and provosts when they join the institution, as their needs may differ from those of the previous administration.

A FEW OTHER WORDS OF WISDOM

Lastly, here are some other words of wisdom that many presidents and provosts would like to share with data professionals. While these pieces of advice do not need much explanation, they are well worth including in this chapter.

- Stay current on the trends in data collection and analysis, and make needed recommendations to the president and provost on how to continually improve the institution's data infrastructure.
- Qualitative data plays an important role in our ability to understand what is going on at our institution. Make sure these types of data are included in collection processes.
- When developing a schedule of data collection activities, make sure to consult with faculty and staff who may have to be involved.
- Don't forget that capturing the student voice should be an important part of many different data projects.

DISCUSSION QUESTIONS

1. What major changes on the horizon will impact data collection and analysis? What are the best ways to communicate these changes to the campus community?
2. This chapter emphasized the need to educate the campus community about how to collect, analyze, and understand data. What are some best practices to follow in this area?
3. Besides posting data on the institution's website and intranet, what are other ways to make data easily accessible to the campus community?
4. What are one to two reports that require the participation of multiple departments to successfully accomplish a comprehensive deliverable? What are some next steps you could take that would allow you to work collaboratively on a single, comprehensive report rather than submitting separate but complementary reports?
5. Think of one large data set that the institution may have. How would that data set be analyzed and presented differently, based on the audience?

REFERENCES

Gagliardi, J. S. & Turk, J. M. (2017). The data-enabled executive: Using analytics for student success and sustainability. Washington, DC: American Council on Education. Retrieved from: www.acenet.edu/news-room/Documents/The-Data-Enabled-Executive.pdf

Soares, L., Gagliardi, J. S., & Nellum, C. J. (2017). The post-traditional learners manifesto revisited: Aligning postsecondary education with real life for adult student success. Washington, DC: American Council on Education. Retrieved from: www.acenet.edu/news-room/Documents/The-Post-Traditional-Learners-Manifesto-Revisited.pdf

Soares, L., Gagliardi, J. S., Wilkinson, P. J., & Hughes, S. L. (2018). Innovative leadership: Insights from the American college president study 2017. Washington, DC: American Council on Education. Retrieved from: www.acenet.edu/news-room/Documents/Innovative-Leadership-Insights-from-the-ACPS-2017.pdf

Soares, L., Steele, P., & Wayt, L. (2016). Evolving higher education business models: Leading with data to deliver results. Washington, DC: American Council on Education. Retrieved from: www.acenet.edu/news-room/Documents/Evolving-Higher-Education-Business-Models.pdf

The Aspen Institute. (2017). Renewal and progress: Strengthening higher education leadership in a time of rapid change. Retrieved from: http://highered.aspeninstitute.org/wp-content/uploads/2017/05/Renewal_Progress_CEP_05122017.pdf

Chapter 9
Faculty Perspectives

Michael S. Harris, Molly K. Ellis, and Kim Nelson Pryor

INTRODUCTION

There is much promise—and just as much risk—in faculty members' drive to create, understand, and effectively utilize data. In an increasingly data-filled world, faculty can and should play an active role. In their varied capacities on higher education campuses, faculty both create their own data and use the qualitative and quantitative data of others to make decisions impacting students, assess student learning, and improve academic programs. This chapter details the multifaceted role faculty play as producers and consumers of data in higher education, as well as related difficulties in faculty participation in data strategy.

First, we provide a brief overview of faculty positions within the higher education landscape, from adjunct and contingent faculty to full-time, tenure-track faculty who may contribute to campus governance, teach diverse groups of students, conduct research, and serve as academic citizens by participating in departmental leadership, campus committees, and professional and scholarly organizations. Then, we describe some of the primary difficulties that faculty face in their academic roles; these include issues common to all faculty, such as time management, as well as issues concerning only certain faculty, such as the highly rigorous tenure and promotion process. Next, we outline the myriad arenas in which faculty utilize both objective and subjective data, relying on it to provide insights into student course performance, for example; to increase knowledge of institutional benchmarking; or to assess personal scholarly production via academic analytics and productivity measures (the latter being a data source that has exploded in popularity in recent years). We then describe common faculty challenges with data, including skepticism concerning the purpose and endgame for solicited data, questions about how data can hurt or help, different conceptualizations of data among administrators and faculty, and issues in accessing and reporting data. We finish the chapter by articulating what faculty want those who create and use data to know.

FACULTY ROLES AND RESPONSIBILITIES

Today's faculty represent a diverse group of scholars, teachers, and researchers with differing motivations for entering academia, varying degrees of participation in the broader campus community, and shifting responsibilities as they navigate the faculty role. While historically a varied role, today's faculty position looks increasingly different across a wide array of higher education institutions—from two-year, vocationally focused community colleges to small, community-oriented liberal arts colleges, to vast research-oriented universities with thriving graduate programs (Harris, 2013). Recent and ongoing changes throughout the field of higher education have only added to the pressures placed on faculty across the spectrum: for adjunct and contingent faculty, who may experience persistent job insecurity, low wages, and lack of oversight and engagement on campus (Bousquet, 2008; Cross & Goldenberg, 2011; Langen, 2011; Rhoades, 1998); for tenure-track faculty, an increasingly grueling tenure process that may leave them feeling pulled in many directions (Alexander, 2000; Eagan & Garvey, 2015; Gappa, Austin, & Trice, 2007; Harris, 2019; Schuster & Finkelstein, 2006; Slaughter & Rhoades, 2004). But before describing in greater detail the difficulties faculty face, we will first review the types of faculty positions and their associated duties.

Faculty are often segmented into two broad categories: non-tenure-track faculty (NTTF) and tenured and tenure-track faculty. Non-tenure-track faculty, who may hold full- or part-time positions, represent a more diverse group than those on the tenure track. Table 9.1 lists sub-types of NTTF.

Once an exception, non-tenure-track positions now dominate higher education, particularly at community colleges and teaching-focused institutions; today, NTTF represent over two-thirds of all higher education faculty (Kezar & Maxey, 2012). While these faculty's diverse roles and varying commitments to

Table 9.1 Sub-Types of Non-Tenure-Track Faculty

Full-Time NTTF	Part-Time NTTF
Teachers	Career enders
Researchers	Specialists, experts, and professionals
Administrators	Aspiring academics
Academic professionals	Freelancers

campus life can complicate institutions' attempts to articulate a data strategy that is equally relevant and accessible to all faculty, we suggest that campus leaders carefully consider the characteristics and needs of their NTTF academic workforce.

For those in more traditional roles (i.e., tenure-track and tenured faculty who are employed full-time at their institution), the faculty position is commonly conceptualized as encompassing three professional pillars: teaching, research, and service. In addition to engaging with students in the campus community through teaching, faculty also advance personal research agendas that include participation in academic associations and conferences and, above all, publishing and disseminating research. Finally, faculty also devote significant time to service, both on and off campus. Each of these three pillars is described in greater detail below.

Teaching

Aside from a small group of faculty assigned exclusively to research or administrative work, the vast majority of faculty teach and advise students. However, *whom* faculty teach varies greatly. Some teach the full range of post-secondary enrollees, from undergraduates up to doctoral students, while others teach only specific levels of students (e.g., graduate students in a particular program). In a similarly various fashion, some faculty teach courses within an institution's general education curriculum, engaging with a broad swath of students from various disciplines, while other faculty teach only highly specialized courses to a select group of students. *When and how often* faculty teach can also differ. Teaching loads vary greatly across types of faculty and institutions, with faculty typically teaching anywhere from two to five classes per semester.

Research

For faculty at research universities, especially those working toward tenure, producing scholarship via research reigns supreme. A promotion to tenure often depends on a faculty member's research productivity, with institutions expecting significant evidence of scholarship from books, journal articles, conference presentations, and external grant activity. In seeing their work through to publication, faculty participate in an array of research-related activities, such as designing studies, learning new research methods, analyzing data, completing IRB applications, and reviewing manuscripts for journals (Harris, 2019). To support these activities, faculty are often encouraged (and at an increasing number of campuses, expected) to secure external funding for research projects; for this reason, grant writing and related responsibilities often occupy a major share of faculty research time. Significant grant expectations, a long-standing feature of many STEM fields, are today more prevalent across almost all departments and disciplines in research universities.

Service

In higher education, faculty not only teach students and undertake research, but also serve as academic citizens (McMillin & Berberet, 2002; Ward, 2003). By participating in peer review and professional associations beyond their home institution, as well as in inter-institutional committee work to hire new faculty, admit students, and oversee curriculum, faculty fundamentally contribute to the effective functioning of higher education (Ward, 2003). Service often takes a back seat to teaching and research—for example, tenure-track faculty may engage only selectively in service activities such as committee or faculty senate work. Other times, service can evolve into fully designated governance or administrative roles, such as when faculty become department chairs or leaders of campus research or academic centers. While such formal service endeavors are often accompanied by release from other teaching and research duties, most service is not; rather, it is an important duty that faculty must undertake in addition to other institutional demands.

DIFFICULTIES FACED BY FACULTY

Across the diverse professional responsibilities of faculty, competing priorities and challenges emerge throughout the stages of the academic career. These difficulties—some of which affect all faculty and others only certain types, or only those at certain institutions—can represent a barrier to, but also an opportunity for, including faculty in an institutional data strategy. Here, we summarize some of the major difficulties faced by those in faculty roles.

Time Management

In today's fast-paced higher education landscape, nearly all faculty face one glaring challenge: time (Berg & Seeber, 2016; Finkelstein, Conley, & Schuster, 2016; Gardner & Veliz, 2014; Plater, 1995; Toutkoushian & Bellas, 1999; Zemsky, Wegner, & Massy, 2005). Whether faculty are juggling the demands of multiple jobs or institutions (as many part-time NTTF do); striving to adequately fulfill teaching, research, and service expectations (as is required on the tenure track); or simply seeking to balance work and life, their time is a precious—and limited—resource. In fact, faculty work and time are best conceptualized as a zero-sum game; time spent on any one task is, by definition, time not spent on another.

While some faculty responsibilities occur on a predictable schedule (e.g., preparing for class and designing syllabi near the start of each semester), most occur all at once. The tasks of advising students, producing research, and participating in campus and disciplinary governance all compete for faculty's time, efforts, and resources. This reality has given rise to advice that all faculty should become "experts in task management" who are able to fill their time with meaningful work (Harris, 2019).

NTTF Difficulties

In addition to the time pressures faced by all faculty, NTTF also face concerns about job security and working conditions. NTTF, particularly those who are employed part-time, can suffer poor institutional treatment. They may experience turbulent employment practices such as last-minute course scheduling and/or cancellation. Additionally, they may receive little support, mentoring, evaluation, or esteem from administrators and colleagues (Cross & Goldenberg, 2011; Langen, 2011). Overall, these NTTF may garner less job stability, fewer benefits, and significantly less pay than full-time, tenure-track faculty (Rhoades & Torres-Olave, 2015). Even full-time NTTF, who have greater access to adequate pay, benefits, and involvement in institutional life, must contend with less secure job conditions than tenured faculty.

Tenure-Track Difficulties

Pre-tenure faculty face unique difficulties as the tenure "clock" ticks. They must fulfill institutional expectations in all three pillars—teaching, research, service—in a high-accountability and timebound context. Institutions, facing pressures from their own external environments, increasingly seek evidence from faculty of demonstrable outcomes such as revenue generation, research production, and more (Gappa et al., 2007). Feeling the crunch, faculty on the tenure track often experience "time famine," which can lead to low job and life satisfaction during this professional period (Perlow, 1999). Collectively, these difficulties represent both a challenge and an opportunity when it comes to involving faculty in institutional efforts to create a data strategy.

FACULTY RELIANCE ON DATA

As trained researchers, scientists, and creators of knowledge, faculty make both daily decisions and longer-term career choices with the aid of various types of data. This data come in forms they themselves seek out and create, as well as in metrics provided by external stakeholders and colleagues. Whatever the source may be, faculty digest and utilize data on a regular basis.

Student-Level Data

Nearly all faculty, particularly those who teach, rely heavily on student-level data. In the classroom, faculty consistently acquire these data through formal and informal avenues, utilizing both formative and summative assessments to measure student progress. Formative assessments provide ongoing feedback on student performance in order to advance students' learning throughout a course. Formative assessment occurs throughout the duration of a course and may include student self-assessment or peer assessment through discussions, writing, quizzes, or other avenues that do not apply to final grades (or at least don't account for the majority of the final grade). Formative assessments help faculty identify problem points or areas of strong content command for some or all students. In this way, instructors may use formative data to evaluate student learning progress, allowing them to adapt instruction if necessary.

In contrast, summative assessments typically occur at the conclusion of an entire course or course unit and are often conducted on a more official basis than formative assessments. Such assessments are graded and heavily weighted in terms of the final course grade. Faculty use summative data to determine if a student has acquired the intended knowledge and skills from the course content. Table 9.2 lists examples of common formative and summative assessments within higher education.

Beyond assessments for student learning, other common types of student-level data take a more subjective, opinion-based form; these include end-of-course evaluations and online instructor reviews from websites, most notably RateMyProfessors.com. In today's climate, faculty may feel pressure or concern regarding students' opinions of their teaching and courses. At many institutions, end-of-course evaluation data serve as the primary—if not sole—source of teaching evaluation data used in tenure, promotion, and contract renewal decisions. Additionally, external review websites or publicly released grade or evaluation data can impact student

Table 9.2 Examples of Formative and Summative Assessments

Formative	Summative
Daily quizzes	End of unit exams
Exit questions	Final exams
Homework assignments	Final papers
Class discussions	Final grades
Reflections	Senior recitals

decisions regarding which courses to take and influence the preconceptions about faculty they bring with them on the first day of class.

Academic Analytics

A mantra of the academic profession is "publish or perish," and many faculty members experience this dictum as constant pressure to produce research output. Moreover, it is not enough to just publish; research faculty must publish scholarship in the "right" journals to make the most impact possible, at least as valued by senior faculty and administrators. Academic institutions, hiring committees, and tenure and promotion committees increasingly rely on citation counts (how often a scholar's work is cited by peers) and journal impact scores (a measure of prestige representing, in part, how often a journal's content is cited by scholars) for submitted work to make hiring and promotion decisions—especially in regard to tenure and, for later-career scholars, promotions to full professor. These types of data are widely utilized as indicators of the rigor and impact of faculty members' research, despite critics' contention that such metrics are flawed and unreliable. In the absence of any other easily quantifiable performance measures for quality of scholarship, they remain the default means of evaluating research quality.

Unsurprisingly, therefore, faculty take metrics like citation counts and journal impact scores into consideration when determining where to publish their research. Such considerations may work in their favor during personnel reviews but may also create a slew of unintended negative consequences for their research. For example, a faculty member may choose to submit an article to a journal that is technically more prestigious (i.e., has a higher impact score) but actually represents less of a good fit for her research. Such a decision puts work at risk of being rejected or failing to reach an appropriate audience—all for the sake of achieving "good" counts. In extreme situations, faculty may let the goal of achieving the "right" numbers supersede all other factors in designing their research agenda and choosing which projects and audiences to target. Ultimately, in both research and teaching, among faculty themselves and those who make important decisions concerning faculty life, problematic but broadly available metrics drive decision making. Moreover, faculty face other data challenges that we address in the next section.

CHALLENGES WITH DATA

There exists a distinct disconnect between the data surrounding faculty members in American higher education and the faculty members themselves. As noted in the previous section, faculty members rely on a variety of data when making daily choices about students and routine choices about their careers. However, as higher education institutions become more accountable to external stakeholders, including state policymakers, students, and parents, faculty are all tasked with producing data from which they do not necessarily reap any benefit, resulting in a data system rife with challenges and questions for faculty.

Shifting Institutional Data Practices

In today's accountability climate, institutional leaders create and rely on data-driven decisions to promote the success of their institutions. Much of this data collection is delegated to internal stakeholders, such as faculty members, to obtain and systematically report. One example is the institutional accreditation process. In the United States, "accreditation is a process of external quality review created and used by higher education to scrutinize colleges, and universities and programs for quality assurance and quality improvement" (Eaton, 2015, p. 1). To meet the demands of accountability, accreditation requires evidence of continuous improvement, especially regarding student learning outcomes, through faculty-driven assessment. The production of data on student learning outcomes relies heavily on the efforts of faculty members, who are left feeling that reporting this data increases their workload with little perceivable benefit. Faculty's lack of clarity on the benefit of these data serves as a root cause of much of the skepticism that attends institutionally solicited data.

Challenge 1: Definition of "Data"

The word "data" can mean many things at different levels of an institution. Thus, one common challenge is the lack of a clear, institution-wide definition of the term. Faculty and their institutions may not share the same view of the importance of various data. What faculty view as important data may differ from the data valued by their institutions. At times, data solicited from faculty by their institution can feel irrelevant and be frustrating to produce. Data managers should consider the clarity and potentially negative perception of data-related terms when creating and communicating a data strategy plan or process with faculty.

Challenge 2: Where Does the Data Go?

When faculty members are asked to report analytics about their courses or students, for instance, they are all too often left out of the loop on the findings and end use of the data. Therefore, producing data can at times feel like tossing work into an abyss, causing faculty to question why they should contribute to such efforts in the first place. To help mitigate this issue, institutional leaders must work purposefully to secure faculty buy-in for the data their institution seeks and ensure that faculty are included in final reporting distributions.

Challenge 3: Perceived Harms of Data

Along the same lines as Challenge 2, a lack of clarity as to the process, purpose, and benefits of data collection may cause faculty to wonder how data can hurt or help them. Faculty reactions to both of these questions can be problematic. If driven by fear, faculty may be hesitant to participate willingly in data collection, drag their feet on fulfilling reporting requirements, or express skepticism and frustration about the value of the data. If driven by perceived benefit, however, faculty may be inclined to produce potentially suspect data that could paint them or their work in a positive light. For example, if an institution wants to see more summative growth in student learning at end-of-course exams, a faculty member may grade less harshly on such an exam for fear that lower grades would reflect poorly on her teaching performance. To counteract such unintended and negative outcomes, institutions should clearly convey how the data that faculty are tasked with producing will be used (and not used) as part of the data strategy process.

Challenge 4: Technology

Typically, institutions today employ online systems or software to help streamline and automate data usage. Often these systems integrate with other institutional systems already in regular use; however, at times they stand alone and necessitate a unique process for data collection. As with all technology, there is a learning curve involved in using data collection software effectively. Therefore, in addition to needing to report data metrics, faculty are tasked with learning software programs that they may only use infrequently. To combat this challenge, institutional leaders and data managers must consider the learning curve inherent to their data collection systems and help faculty get up to speed as quickly as possible.

Challenge 5: Overreliance on Quantitative Data

Much of the data solicited by institutional leaders and external stakeholders is traditionally "grounded in quantitative measurements that emphasize percentages and benchmarks because they are easy to collect, interpret and distribute" (Contreras-McGavin & Kezar, 2007, p. 70). Accountability systems often require measurable (i.e., numeric) metrics to prove success. However, not all the work that faculty do to aid student learning can be captured with a number. Nor can all classroom learning be represented—much less analyzed—quantitatively. Qualitative measures, such as firsthand student accounts of coursework or reflections on institutional curricula, may be useful for a more holistic understanding of student learning successes and shortcomings.

In sum, it is important to note that faculty of all ranks and positions face challenges with data. Those described above, rooted in the all too common uncertainty and lack of clarity surrounding the use and purpose of data, can be experienced by faculty in any role. Institutions can alleviate much faculty stress concerning data through carefully crafted communication and education, as well as purposeful efforts to include faculty voices when determining what types of data are valued.

THE FACULTY PERSPECTIVE ON IMPROVING DATA STRATEGY

For many faculty, their scholarly lifeblood is creating and disseminating data. Yet when it comes to the data that informs their activities and those of their institution, they quickly become disenchanted. As we have detailed throughout this chapter, there are numerous areas where data can improve the work of faculty, but many challenges remain. If campus leaders can properly address these challenges, faculty can become some of the strongest supporters of an effective data strategy and framework. In this section, we detail the faculty perspective on how to improve data management, collection, and utilization.

Faculty are predisposed to support data collection and use. From their graduate training and socialization onward into their careers, faculty across disciplines use data in their teaching and research. So what causes faculty to become skeptical of and frustrated with data, and what can be done to mitigate this problem? First, data managers must understand and appreciate the ubiquitous faculty experience of data fatigue. The majority of data systems, dashboards, and data visualization platforms require tedious data entry on the part of faculty. Today, more than at any other point in the history of higher education, faculty are asked to provide a nearly constant stream of data on their students as well as on their own activities. As scholars and teachers on the frontlines of much of an institution's mission-critical work, faculty are often the first and best source sought out to provide data. However, data managers must be aware that every office on campus wants information from faculty. Student affairs wants data on student conduct and concerns. The retention office wants information on students who might be considering leaving the institution. The IT department wants faculty feedback on any number of new software tools they are considering.

Each of these data requests is reasonable and serves positive goals. Objectively, many faculty even agree on their usefulness. But being bombarded by a never-ending series of data requests from all corners of campus can wear down even the most responsive of faculty members. When opportunities for data requests arise, data managers should determine—before resorting to pitching faculty—if they can get the data by other means. If the desired data does not have another viable source, they should undertake in-depth discussions and perhaps seek multiple levels of approval before asking faculty to report additional data. In an ideal world, an office would be unable to submit a request for data from faculty without concurrently identifying another area of data reporting to remove. Often, data requestors only consider the reporting burden of their immediate request (*This survey will only take five minutes*, they say), yet the cumulative burden and administrative fatigue faced by faculty as data requests compound each other not only increases faculty frustrations but also impairs the overall use of data on campus.

In addition to addressing the realities of data fatigue, data managers must commit to "closing the loop" on the insights gained from the data. Even as the number of surveys, data requests, and reporting requirements confronting them exponentially increase, faculty rarely get to see the results. Consider this: does the student affairs division commonly share data on student conduct or the number of successful interventions they were able to create thanks to faculty data? Does the retention office discuss strategies with faculty and communicate how faculty data helps to improve retention? Does the department of information technology publicize their survey results and reveal how their decision to purchase a certain software tool will improve the problems faculty identified?

To state the obvious, faculty will be more likely to fulfill data requests if they see results and tangible actions taken from previous requests. Given the avalanche of requests and growing administrative burdens placed on faculty, data managers must commit to sharing results and, even more critically, communicating *actions* demonstrating that compiling data are worth faculty time. Too often, faculty are forced to enter data that flows into a pretty dashboard but is never effectively used to make decisions. This wasted time proves frustrating and unproductive for everyone.

Moreover, data managers and administrators often become exasperated with faculty who "retreat" behind academic freedom, raise privacy concerns, or generally express distrust over the use of data. To be sure, these concerns are sometimes legitimate and sometimes not. In many cases, however, such concerns are rooted in a lack of transparency regarding how the data will be used and what decisions might be made in light of their findings. Data managers must understand the current forces from both inside and outside of higher education that contribute to data skepticism, fear, and hostility on the part of faculty. Faculty often feel pressured to do more with less (fewer resources, less time, etc.). Their concerns regarding how data are used, especially in regard to personnel evaluation, are therefore more reasonable than they may seem at first glance. One of the best and easiest ways to assuage faculty concerns is by providing upfront and transparent information regarding how data will be used. In the absence of clear information within the current higher education environment of high stakes accountability, faculty may assume nefarious purposes or negative outcomes regardless of the intent behind a data request.

Finally, there are two keys to achieving a successful data strategy. The first is to build partnerships within a campus culture where faculty are key participants. In order to accomplish this, data managers must understand the need to communicate, share an inspiring vision, and provide clear rationales for the use of data on campus. Second, faculty recognitions and evaluations should reward the time and effort faculty invest in data collection and reporting. Over time, these key approaches will promote data usage and bring faculty into the process as supporters and partners.

CONCLUSION

In the current environment, faculty face a variety of pressures and changing work conditions. The decline of tenure-track positions, increases in part-time faculty, and institutional desires for greater faculty productivity can present challenges for incorporating faculty into a healthy data strategy on campus. Furthermore, while faculty roles vary significantly across institutional types, these increasing pressures exist throughout higher education. Yet faculty still rely on data for many aspects of their jobs, especially their work with students, and can become strong partners and avid supporters of a campus data culture. By bringing faculty into the process, demonstrating the use and purpose of data, and creating actionable results, institutional leaders, researchers, and data managers can achieve this. Ultimately, a successful data strategy relies on robust faculty participation to meet the internal and external demands for data facing higher education for the foreseeable future.

DISCUSSION QUESTIONS

1. As more and more faculty in higher education assume part-time positions or roles off the tenure track, how have you seen this trend impact your institution?

2. The teaching, research, and service roles of faculty can look quite different depending on the type of college or university. How do you think these differences influence the day-to-day work of faculty at your institution?
3. In this chapter, we discuss multiple types of student-level data, including assessments of all kinds; what types of student data do you believe are most helpful for faculty?
4. Identify which of the five data challenges in this chapter is most important to improving data strategy. Name three concrete steps that might help mitigate this challenge.
5. Faculty often feel a sense of data fatigue from: (a) too many requests, and (b) a consistent failure of data managers to "close the loop" and share results. In your view, which of these two causes of fatigue presents the bigger problem?
6. Two keys to a successful data strategy when working with faculty are building partnerships and creating a supportive campus culture. How can data managers work to achieve these goals?

REFERENCES

Alexander, F. K. (2000). The changing face of accountability: Monitoring and assessing institutional performance in higher education. *Journal of Higher Education*, 71(4), 411–431.

Berg, M., & Seeber, B. (2016). *The slow professor: Challenging the culture of speed in the academy*. Toronto: University of Toronto Press.

Bousquet, M. (2008). *How the university works: Higher education and the low-wage nation*. New York: NYU Press.

Contreras-McGavin, M., & Kezar, A. (2007). Using qualitative methods to assess student learning in higher education. *New Directions for Institutional Research*, 2007(136), 69–79.

Cross, J. G., & Goldenberg, E. N. (2011). *Off-track profs: Nontenured teachers in higher education*. Cambridge, MA: MIT Press.

Eagan, K. J., & Garvey, J. C. (2015). Stressing out: Connecting race, gender, and stress with faculty productivity. *Journal of Higher Education*, 86(6), 923–954.

Eaton, J. S. (2015). *An overview of US accreditation*. Retrieved from www.chea.org/overview-us-accreditation

Finkelstein, M. J., Conley, V. M., & Schuster, J. H. (2016). *The faculty factor: Reassessing the American academy in a turbulent era*. Baltimore, MD: Johns Hopkins University Press.

Gappa, J. M., Austin, A. E., & Trice, A. G. (2007). *Rethinking faculty work: Higher education's strategic imperative*. San Francisco, CA: Jossey-Bass.

Gardner, S. K., & Veliz, D. (2014). Evincing the ratchet: A thematic analysis of the promotion and tenure guidelines at a striving university. *Review of Higher Education*, *38*(1), 105–132.

Harris, M. S. (2013). *Understanding institutional diversity in American higher education*. San Francisco, CA: Jossey-Bass.

Harris, M. S. (2019). *How to get tenure: Strategies for successfully navigating the process*. New York: Routledge.

Kezar, A., & Maxey, D. (2012). Missing from the institutional data picture: Non-tenure track faculty. *New Directions for Institutional Research*, *155*, 47–65.

Langen, J. M. (2011). Evaluation of adjunct faculty in higher education institutions. *Assessment & Evaluation in Higher Education*, *36*(2), 185–196.

McMillin, L. A., & Berberet, W. G. (Eds.). (2002). *A new academic compact: Revisioning the relationship between faculty and their institutions*. Bolton, MA: Anker.

Perlow, L. A. (1999). The time famine: Towards a sociology of work. *Administrative Science Quarterly*, *44*(1), 57–81.

Plater, W. M. (1995). Future work faculty time in the 21st century. *Change: The Magazine of Higher Learning*, *27*(3), 22–33.

Rhoades, G. (1998). *Managed professionals: Unionized faculty and restructuring academic labor*. Albany, NY: State University of New York.

Rhoades, G., & Torres-Olave, B. M. (2015). Academic capitalism and (secondary) academic labor markets: Negotiating a new academy and research agenda. In M. B. Paulsen (Ed.), *Higher education: Handbook of theory and research* (pp. 383–430). Dordrecht, Netherlands: Springer.

Schuster, J. H., & Finkelstein, M. (2006). *The American faculty: The restructuring of academic work and careers*. Baltimore, MD: Johns Hopkins University Press.

Slaughter, S., & Rhoades, G. (2004). *Academic capitalism and the new economy: Markets, state, and higher education*. Baltimore, MD: Johns Hopkins University Press.

Toutkoushian, R. K., & Bellas, M. L. (1999). Faculty time allocations and research productivity: Gender, race and family effects. *Review of Higher Education*, *22*(4), 367–390.

Ward, K. (2003). *Faculty service roles and the scholarship of engagement*. San Francisco, CA: Jossey-Bass.

Zemsky, R., Wegner, G. R., & Massy, W. F. (2005). *Remaking the American university: Market-smart and mission-centered*. New Brunswick, NJ: Rutgers University Press.

Chapter 10
Student Affairs Leaders' Perspectives

Sheri Jones

INTRODUCTION

Students are the largest group of decision makers at an institution of higher education. Providing leaders with tools and information to make informed decisions is critical and does not happen by accident. It occurs with a thorough understanding of an institution's student population and collaborating with multiple departments simultaneously to support student success. This chapter offers some insights into the current challenges facing student affairs leaders as consumers of data.

Student affairs leaders play a significant role in developing programs and services to promote student success, and they rely on data to ensure that they provide the most impactful offerings. For the purposes of this chapter, the term "student affairs" or "student services" shall be expanded to encompass the use of data to influence any services that support a student's higher education journey outside of the classroom or their specific program of study. Regardless of the area of service, hearts are generally in the right place when it comes to student support programs. However, ideas will range from being based almost fully on data or information to being based on tribal knowledge; from an educated deduction drawing on the experience and expertise of the champion to a simple hunch about "the right thing to do." The best decisions are those that incorporate all of the above.

Sometimes an initiative for enhanced support services stems from tribal or experience-based knowledge and needs to be tested through an analysis of related data or through a pilot study with a subset of the population for whom it is intended. In these cases, the initiative can be shaped by the data drawn upon to support or refute the concept. An idea based on sound reasoning and experience is most often neither supported nor refuted, but is shaped in different ways based on data analyses.

At other times, an initiative can be formed in just the opposite way. Data analyses, a review of regular reports, or even a pilot study to review an idea can indicate a need for changes or enhancements to services. In these cases, ideation stems from information gleaned through more formal data, and then expertise, experience, and instincts come into play when developing appropriate improvements, interventions, or enhancements.

To make the best decisions, nobody should work in a vacuum inside or outside of student affairs. Sharing best practices, ideas, and data cross-functionally will yield better results than looking at each type of information in a silo. After all, the student learner is a whole person operating within the context of his or her experiences, opportunities, and obstacles across the institution and outside of it. No one service, intervention, or learning opportunity will have the same effect on each student, each group of students, or all students within a population.

This chapter begins with a description of student affairs positions before discussing difficult components of the position, which serves as an important backdrop to discuss data issues and strategies. The reliance on data by student affairs professionals and our current challenges are described before addressing key points that we (student affairs leaders) want data people to know in order to help move the student success and institutional-effectiveness needle.

BRIEF DESCRIPTION OF STUDENT AFFAIRS POSITIONS

Depending on the college or university, there are quite a few functional areas that may fall under the "student affairs" or "student services" umbrella. Traditionally, divisions/departments of student affairs have been home to a selection of co-curricular activities and services. In keeping with the dynamic and individualistic nature of higher education, functional areas under the student affairs umbrella vary by institution and also fluctuate within a given institution.

The National Association of Student Personnel Administrators (NASPA) Research and Policy Institute turned to chief student affairs officers at colleges and universities across the United States to get a better understanding of which functional areas make up the student affairs divisions at their respective institutions (Wesaw & Sponsler, 2014). The NASPA survey found that the following 12 functional areas fell under the purview of the division of student affairs at least two-thirds of responding institutions:

- Campus Activities (98% of responding institutions)
- Student Conduct/Case Management (behavioral) (97%)

- Counseling Services (89%)
- Orientation (88%)
- Student Affairs Assessment (80%)
- Career Services (73%)
- Student Conduct/Academic Integrity (72%)
- Wellness Programs (70%)
- Disability Support Services (70%)
- On-Campus Housing (69%)
- Recreational Sports (66%)
- Multicultural Services (66%).

The following functions are the most commonly housed within a division of student affairs; there are many others that an institution may include as well. Depending on the size and structure of the institution, any function that provides support for students outside of the classroom may be included in the division of student affairs. These may include, but are not limited to:

- Community Service/Service Learning
- Health Programs
- Enrollment Management/Admissions
- Student Unions
- Financial Aid
- Campus Safety
- Academic Support Services.

(Wesaw & Sponsler, 2014)

Divisions of student affairs are generally led by a senior-level administrator who reports directly to the institution's president. The chief student affairs officer often holds the title of vice president or dean. These administrators spend the majority of their time working on internal institutional activities, such as interacting with students, crisis management, personnel management, and strategic planning (Wesaw & Sponsler, 2014).

The work of the chief student affairs officer is supported by staff. Depending on the size and structure of the institution, functional areas are likely to have their own leadership teams, including department heads and supervisors, as well as frontline professional and student staff engaging in day-to-day operations (Pritchard & McChesney, 2018). Frontline staff make up the majority of the employees in a division of student affairs.

DIFFICULT COMPONENTS OF STUDENT AFFAIRS LEADERSHIP POSITIONS

Like all departments in higher education institutions, student affairs has its share of difficulties. The most challenging aspect of managing a department of student affairs may very well be figuring out the right services, programs, or interventions to provide at the right time and to the right students. The ever-shifting nature of student demographics makes the appropriate delivery of interventions even trickier. Add to that the endless swell of new initiatives and the tightening of budgets, and it's easy to see how student affairs departments can become overwhelmed.

Changing Student Demographics

Changing student demographics is one of the top issues of concern cited by chief student affairs officers in a recent survey (Wesaw & Sponsler, 2014). Arguably, it is not necessarily the demographic *shift* that is the problem, but rather the *spread*. The data tells us that students we have now (and those we expect to support in the near future) are older; are racially, ethnically, and culturally more diverse; and have a wider range of life circumstances, such as employment and dependent care responsibilities, than students before (Lumina Foundation, 2019). This spread of student characteristics means it's not enough to just offer different programs, services, and initiatives; we must offer more guided pathways, aimed at supporting students across the board (College and University Personnel Administrators, 2018). Having sufficient information becomes a moving target as student populations and needs continually change.

In response to these demographic changes, student affairs leaders attempt to develop new programs, offer new services, and create full-scale initiatives in our quest to make sure no student falls through the cracks. Often, before the data has even been collected on the latest program, we find ourselves huddled around the conference table poring over issues and brainstorming initiatives to address them. As we strive to meet the needs of all of our students, we start to experience fatigue brought on by the confusion and exhaustion of constantly adding new programs, services, and initiatives (Kuh & Hutchings, 2015). And, of course, each new program, service, and initiative requires data collection, analysis, and assessment.

A 24/7 College or University

Along with juggling this smorgasbord of services, programs, and initiatives, student affairs professionals struggle with answering the question, "What is a timely response?" in today's 24/7 world, where we are always connected to email, texts, and social media. Providing all services around the clock is unrealistic from a personnel and cost perspective. Rather, the goal should be to evaluate and balance what is best for the entire community, including students, alumni, faculty, staff, donors, and board members with what is affordable and realistic within fiscal constraints. It is about finding the sweet spot.

Of course, none of this is happening in a vacuum; it's occurring in an environment where budgets seem to be constantly tightening (Understanding Key Challenges in Student Affairs). While institutions strive to use data and assessment to evaluate and improve their programs, finding the time and space to review the data across programs and step back and look for opportunities to gain synergy across programs may be challenging (Kuh & Hutchings, 2015).

Competing Stakeholder Priorities

Any organization has a myriad of stakeholders to please both internally and externally, but an institution of higher education may be among the most complex systems in this regard. Internally, there are students, alumni, faculty, staff, and a board of directors. Externally, there are the education community, including accreditors, the directly served communities where prospective students live and alumni work, employers, donors, education partners, the general public, and numerous local, state and federal regulators, and interested entities, including those who provide financial aid funding to students of the institution. All of these stakeholders have an interest in improved student outcomes and view support programs through slightly to largely different lenses, depending on the issue being addressed.

For example, everyone expects fiscal responsibility; you must operate within the means of the institution. However, some stakeholders want money to be directed toward the mission, while others want to advance their own group's priorities. Students want right-place, right-time services. And there is generally a need to appeal to one or more external stakeholder groups. At the end of the day, student affairs leadership will be looking for impact (effectiveness) at the lowest possible cost (efficiency). Simply put, they want to do more for students but have limited resources at their disposal.

Student affairs leaders require data to justify the use of resources needed to develop, maintain, and grow programs. To garner support, they often have to be prepared to defend programming to a multitude of audiences. With so many competing priorities involved, programs need to appeal to the broadest possible spectrum of stakeholders, and data strategies need to consider each group not only independently, but also collectively when making recommendations to senior leaders. This does not mean that data should be artificially adjusted or altered, nor that facts that do not support an initiative be covered or hidden. But keeping the audience in mind and leading with solid information that will garner support for programs that have been proven effective is simply good leadership. For example, if a program has been proven to be more cost-effective than an alternative and leads to better student outcomes, then lead with the finances to appeal to the finance and budgeting department, and lead with student outcomes to appeal to the dean of the school where you want support for expanding the program.

RELIANCE ON DATA

Chief student affairs officers, student affairs leaders, and frontline staff are expected to rely on data for decision making support. Leadership must balance great ideas, research, data collection, data analysis, and reports with the need to make solid choices regarding how to use resources. In order to pull together a complete picture, decision makers rely on data both from external sources, such as benchmarking against other institutions, and from internal sources, such as student success analyses.

Commitment to Using Data

A landscape analysis undertaken by NASPA, the Association for Institutional Research (AIR), and EDUCAUSE found that institutions are using both descriptive and predictive student success studies in their decision making. Divisions of student affairs rely on this data to make decisions about improving student outcomes from interventions, more efficiently delivering programs and services, and eliminating or reducing programs and services that do not contribute significantly to student success (Parnell, Jones, Wesaw, & Brooks, 2018). As institutions become more reliant on descriptive and predictive data for decision making, they may start to shift toward building a culture of evidence, where departmental staff at every level understand the type of evidence necessary to garner support for new ideas. Creating an environment where a culture of evidence thrives requires commitment and support from student affairs leadership (Balser, Grabau, Kniess, & Page, 2017).

Digging into the Data to Make Informed Decisions

When presented with new opportunities, a leader in any position would love to say, "Let's do it!" to every great-sounding idea, to each request for programs, to all requests for additional staff. Unfortunately, that is not realistic. Instead, leadership must figure out the sweet spot: the pieces of information

> - Who are the students and how many will participate/be impacted?
> - What are the expected outcomes from implementation?
> - What resources will be needed?
> - What are the program logistics?
>   - Will it be in-person or online?
>   - Will it be self-service or will there be facilitation?
>   - Will a facility be needed?
> - When is the program or intervention needed within the student life cycle?
> - Why is the program intervention needed?
> - How long will the program take to develop?
> - How much will the program cost?

FIGURE 10.1 Data Strategy Questions for Consideration When Proposing Initiatives

needed to make the right decisions at the right time, defend and implement those decisions, and measure the success of those decisions.

Simply put, leadership must identify the who, what, where, when, why, and how for each initiative. The more the who, what, where, when, why, and how can be supported or even driven by data, the more likely student affairs leaders will be to buy into the idea, and the better equipped they will be to present the idea, which sometimes means defending it or convincing others to back it. Figure 10.1 includes some data strategy questions that chief student affairs leaders think about; readers may wish to consider these when presenting new programs and services.

In addition to needing data for wholistic decision making, student affairs professionals require access to comprehensive data for broad campus efforts, such as initiative and program assessments, strategic planning, and accreditation (regional and programmatic) (Fallucca, 2017). Given the ever-expanding breadth and depth of data required to meet the needs of such varied stakeholders, colleges and universities will benefit from looking for efficiencies in how they collect, analyze, and report data. Developing a strategy that looks across analysis and reporting needs allows institutions to make the most of their data resources.

CURRENT CHALLENGES IN GETTING AND USING DATA

To answer any or all of the who, what, where, when, why, and how questions described in the previous section, data or information is needed. Some data may be easily accessible and require little to no analytics, reporting, or research. Conversely, some of it may be more difficult to obtain and may require extensive research, multiple reports, and complicated analytics. Student affairs professionals may also face other challenges in efficiently and

STUDENT AFFAIRS LEADERS' PERSPECTIVES

FIGURE 10.2 Current Challenges in Getting and Using Data

effectively obtaining and using data. Figure 10.2 shows seven current challenges in getting and using data; a description of each follows.

Time

As with any higher education initiative, finding the right balance of time and effort to spend on data collection, analysis, and reporting for a positive return on that investment can be a challenge. Often, spending time on data activities means taking staff time from elsewhere. For example, suppose frontline career services staff have been asked to track and report their time spent on providing students with different services, such as career advising, career assessments, resumé support, and job-application assistance. While recording their activities, calculating totals, and reporting that data, the career services professional is unavailable to directly provide career services to students. Care should be taken to establish an appropriate balance so that service delivery does not suffer at the expense of data analysis.

Time can also be an issue insofar as it is a finite resource. When asked to identify the amount of time they spend on strategic planning activities, chief student affairs officers estimated 12% on average. When asked what the ideal amount of time to dedicate to such activities would be, they indicated that they would prefer to spend closer to 18% of their time on strategic planning (Wesaw & Sponsler, 2014).

Buy-In

As a division of student affairs moves to become increasingly data driven in its decision making, leaders may find that they have to pause along the way to make sure everyone is along for the ride. Increased assessment activities

149

can elicit fear or skepticism in staff who perceive these efforts as regulatory, as opposed to transformational (Fuller & Lane, 2017). Fuller and Lane's research found that, of survey respondents, nearly *half* agreed with the statement "The majority of student affairs staff in my division are afraid of assessment." Student affairs administrators must work to shift staff perceptions by emphasizing the internal continuous-improvement aspects of data collection and analysis, rather than external stakeholders and reporting.

Further, moving from simply increasing assessment to cultivating an evidence-based culture involves additional work. A true cultural shift requires buy-in beyond the division of student affairs. The division can work toward this by engaging other stakeholders and departments, aligning assessment priorities with institutional goals and priorities, and mapping out a clear communication strategy for working with campus partners (Balser, Grabau, Kniess, & Page, 2017).

Training

Of course, convincing student affairs staff of the merits of data collection, analysis, and reporting will not do much good without also bringing them up to speed on how to carry out these efforts. Training can be a hurdle to a productive data strategy. In some cases, training will be directed at existing student affairs staff to teach them the necessary software, methodology, analytical skills, and reporting techniques (Ro, Menard, Kniess, & Nickelsen, 2017). Alternatively, if the institutional research or assessment staff will complete the bulk of the data work, they may require training in student affairs practices and terminology to create effective measurement tools. In addition, cross-training may be required to allow for productive communication between the departments.

Initiative Fatigue

While developing and implementing a data strategy for student affairs is certainly important, so are all of the *other* critical initiatives that staff are already committed to implementing and maintaining. Adding yet another "top priority" can lead to some staff feeling overwhelmed and confused about which activities should take precedence (Kuh & Hutchings, 2015). Initiative fatigue is often the result of staff not seeing the connections between the work and the assessment; that is, the assessment of their work feels like one more thing they have to do instead of an integral component of the program or initiative.

Data Quality

A large-scale increase in the breadth and depth of data collected, stored, and analyzed for advanced assessment necessarily comes with additional concerns about the quality of the data. Often, analysis of student affairs outcomes requires self-reported survey data, which creates reliability challenges that must be addressed. In order to complete the desired types of analyses, datasets may be combined, requiring a certain level of skill and familiarity with the data to be validated (Ro, Menard, Kniess, & Nickelsen, 2017). Concerns about data quality can be compounded by concerns about adequate training of data users, discussed above.

Data Quantity

The more data you can access and present as useful and relevant information to a stakeholder, the more questions arise. Each leader has to figure out how much data are enough (or where the sweet spot is) within the context of the organization, needs, and decision making structures. A researcher needs to spend time working with leadership and offering information, as well as learning about an institution and its students, to hit a stride with the production of data. It can be a frustrating but rewarding journey that can lead to greater credibility and the opportunity to see data turned into action that fosters student development and learning.

Data Requests

Once it becomes widely known that data, reports, and analyses are available, the questions may start to fly! While this is a good thing, it can also drown the frequently under-resourced student affairs professional in a sea of nice-to-have data requests and curiosity questions. In today's higher education economy, institutional research offices are often stretched thin and therefore cannot afford to indulge existential questions for the sake of knowledge or go down rabbit holes that lead nowhere. Falling back on the who, what, where, when, why, and how questions can help discern which requests have the highest potential value to the institution and keep focus and resources directed toward them.

WHAT WE REALLY WANT DATA PEOPLE TO UNDERSTAND

Leaders want to know that they can trust the information that is produced within their organization; have it delivered in a concise and useful form; and have follow-up questions answered specifically, succinctly, and quickly. Easy, right? From any leader's perspective, it should be. But those people tasked with producing the information know that isn't often the case. Let's review each part separately for clarity.

Trusting the Information

The last thing anyone wants to do is make a decision based on faulty information. Upon receiving a report, leaders immediately look at the numbers and begin digesting the information. They trust that the analyses and calculations have been done correctly. When leaders skip over the methodology section, it is not because they aren't interested in that portion but because they trust the researcher who did the work. Leaders may not always understand why it takes so long to get information, but at the end of the day everyone wants to get data they can rely on, regardless of the consequences to the timeline.

Deliver in Stages Rather than Miss a Deadline

Missing a deadline is less than ideal. Time gets away from all of us. Emergency situations come up, and projects take longer than expected due to unforeseen circumstances. However, rather than missing a deadline entirely, try one of these intermediate steps:

- Give them something. Deliver a reliable data nugget if you have one, and update on progress. Above all, deliver information and solutions, not excuses. But don't give them early indications that have not been through some level of quality assurance. If you provide early indications that are later determined to be incorrect, you may have done more harm than good.
- Provide relevant information, even if it is not the end game. But don't provide irrelevant information or fluff. Most leaders will see through this, and you will end up seeming like you don't understand the question or, even worse, your own work.
- Let them know early that you may miss the deadline and troubleshoot regarding alternative information that may suffice in the interim. Give them alternatives and solutions, not open-ended problems. Provide a framework for delivery if the timeframe is going to slip. If you need extra time, resources, or access to make a deadline, be clear about what will expedite and facilitate your good work.

Spend the Most Time on Action Discussion

There is a tendency for data analysts to spend most of a 30-minute meeting on data methodology and limitations. If you are a data analyst, talking about the data details is exciting and comfortable. However, senior leaders want to spend the majority of the time exploring ways to enhance the student

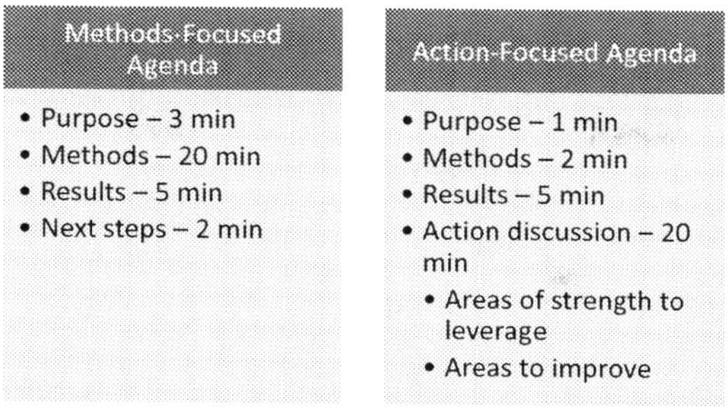

STUDENT AFFAIRS LEADERS' PERSPECTIVES

Methods-Focused Agenda
- Purpose – 3 min
- Methods – 20 min
- Results – 5 min
- Next steps – 2 min

Action-Focused Agenda
- Purpose – 1 min
- Methods – 2 min
- Results – 5 min
- Action discussion – 20 min
  - Areas of strength to leverage
  - Areas to improve

FIGURE 10.3 Methods-Focused vs Action-Focused Agendas

experience. Figure 10.3 shows two different agendas for the same 30-minute meeting. The "methods-focused agenda" is fairly common but offers the least time for senior leaders' greatest interest—taking action on the data. The "action-focused agenda" allows for richer discussion on actions that could be taken to improve student success based on the data presented.

DISCUSSION QUESTIONS

1. Of the current challenges in getting and using data that were discussed in the chapter, select two. What solutions would you offer to data strategists? Describe each solution. What are the limitations or downsides to each recommended solution?
2. Of the student affairs offices listed in this chapter, which two do you know the most and least about? Why? What value would be added to your current or intended role by learning more about the two that you know least about?
3. Assume you have completed a study that deems a pilot program successful on most outcome measures. The vice president of student affairs has asked you to provide data points and a related rationale that support expansion of the program to a broader group of students. What questions will you want to ask before providing the requested information? Why?
4. Your supervisor asked you to work on a time-sensitive project and you underestimated the time it would take to complete the analysis. When and how would you break the news to your supervisor?

REFERENCES

Balser, T. J., Grabau, A. A., Kniess, D., & Page, L. A. (2017). Collaboration and communication. *New Directions for Institutional Research*, *2017*(175), pp. 65–79. Retrieved from: https://onlinelibrary.wiley.com/doi/epdf/10.1002/ir.20236

College and University Personnel Administrators. (2018). Focus on student affairs, 2018: Understanding key challenges using CUPA-HR data. Retrieved from www.cupahr.org/wp-content/uploads/Student_Affairs_Report.pdf

Fallucca, A. (2017). Student affairs assessment, strategic planning, and accreditation. *New Directions for Institutional Research*, *2017*(175), pp. 89–102. Retrieved from: https://onlinelibrary.wiley.com/doi/epdf/10.1002/ir.20238

Fuller, M. B., & Lane, F. C. (2017). An empirical model of culture of assessment in student affairs. *Research & Practice in Assessment*, *12*, pp. 18–27. Retrieved from: https://files.eric.ed.gov/fulltext/EJ1168691.pdf

Kuh, G. D., & Hutchings, P. (2015). Initiative fatigue: Keeping the focus on learning. In G. D. Kuh (Ed.), *Using evidence of student learning to improve higher education* (pp. 183–200). San Francisco, CA: Jossey-Bass.

Lumina Foundation. (2019). Lumina foundation today's student infographic 2019. Retrieved from: www.luminafoundation.org/todays-student

Parnell, A., Jones, D., Wesaw, A., & Brooks, D. C. (2018). *Institutions' use of data and analytics for student success: Results from a national landscape analysis*. Washington, DC: NASPA – Student Affairs Administrators in Higher Education, the Association for Institutional Research, and EDUCAUSE. Retrieved from: www.naspa.org/rpi/reports/data-and-analytics-for-student-success

Pritchard, A., & McChesney, J. (2018). Focus on student affairs, 2018: Understanding key challenges using CUPA-HR data. Knoxville, TN: College and University Professional Association for Human Resources (CUPA-HR). Retrieved from: www.cupahr.org/wp-content/uploads/Student_Affairs_Report.pdf

Ro, H. K., Menard, T., Kniess, D., & Nickelsen, A. (2017). New(er) methods and tools in student affairs assessment. *New Directions for Institutional Research*, *2017* (175), pp. 49–63. Retrieved from: https://onlinelibrary.wiley.com/doi/epdf/10.1002/ir.20235

Wesaw, A. J., & Sponsler, A. (2014). *The chief student affairs officer*. Washington, DC: NASPA-Student Affairs Administrators in Higher Education. Retrieved from: www.naspa.org/images/uploads/main/CSAO_2014_ExecSum_Download2.pdf

Chapter 11

Institutional Researchers' Perspectives

Erez Lenchner

INTRODUCTION

The scope of work of institutional researchers, as well as their relations with internal and external stakeholders, has changed dramatically since the inception of the field. The most significant changes have taken place over the last 15 years of the field's 60 years. As information has become more and more widely distributed, consumed, and interpreted, institutional research (IR) has become less and less siloed. Students, faculty, and staff members previously seen as data consumers (or "clients") are now viewed as decision makers who analyze, interpret, and utilize IR data on their own (Swing & Ross, 2016a). These changes have coincided with changes in technology, college structures, and the training of researchers and data consumers.

BRIEF DESCRIPTION OF INSTITUTIONAL RESEARCH

The positions of IR professionals regarding their core roles coincide with changes in the data structures and information spheres across the higher education sector. Historically, IR work has been limited by the legacy information systems available to colleges and universities. Information has been mostly archival and snapshot based, providing the basis for regulatory (largely retrospective) reports on student outcomes. Over time, IR has been assigned responsibility for knowledge management, commonly defined as processes used to gather and transform data into information and knowledge, as well as "to collaborate in the creation and maintenance of an institutional official repository of data, information, and knowledge." (Serban, 2002, p. 106; Volkwein, 1999, p. 17). Indeed, to date, roles currently reported across all IR offices include primary responsibility for data reporting (accreditation, state and federal agencies), institutional fact books, enrollment reporting and analysis (Swing & Ross, 2016a). In a recent review, Webber (2018) provides detailed mapping of the historical definitions of IR, highlighting three common function areas: institutional reporting, data analysis, and data interpretation.

In diligently balancing archival (or regulatory) reporting and forecasting analysis aimed at improving institutional effectiveness, IR professionals still report a greater workload within the reporting component. This is due to IR's responsibility for providing data to internal and external stakeholders while also supporting users in interpreting and understanding those data. IR has thus taken on a "holistic" role, one that merges the responsibilities of a data archivist with those of an analyst, a researcher, and a policymaker.

To accomplish this multifaceted role, IR needs to be well positioned in an institution or a college/university system. While the definition of a well-positioned function will vary across institutions, IR professionals need to be positioned where they are empowered to help frame research questions, set the direction for analysis, and support the crafting of policy recommendations. Irrespective of its assignment in a campus organizational chart, IR should be an integral part of a campus's decision making group for both short- and long-term policies.

DIFFICULT COMPONENTS OF IR POSITIONS

Competing Priorities and Stakeholders

Institutional researchers face ongoing changes in the technological working environment and in the demand for information. Concurrently, they face an ever-growing need to educate users regarding the process of crafting research questions applicable to a college or university setting. The reliance on users to elaborate their research needs has increased with the exponential growth of data resources. At the same time, IR professionals now have to provide senior executives, faculty, and staff with instructions about the underlying components of a research design that cannot be developed simply with additional access to computing power or modern information systems.

Educational Data Mining

The work environment of institutional researchers has also been affected by the practice of educational data mining (EDM), which has been experiencing near-exponential growth (Baker, Pechenizkiy, Romero, & Ventura, 2010; Berland, Baker, & Blikstein, 2014; Heiner, Heffernan, & Barnes, 2007; Junco & Cotten, 2011; Luan, 2007; Peña-Ayala, 2013, 2014; Romero & Ventura, 2010). Methods of academic analytics and data mining dating back only to around the year 2000 (Luan, 2002; Heiner et al., 2007; Peña-Ayala, 2013, 2014) have vastly expanded the ability of college researchers to compile, analyze, and draw associations from student-level administrative records. As a set of new techniques, "Educational Data Mining is an emerging discipline, concerned with developing methods for exploring the unique types of data that come from educational settings, and using those methods to better understand students, and the settings in which they learn" (Baker & Yacef, 2009, p. 4).

The data mining process changes the work of institutional researchers, as it starts by gathering live and historical data stored in information systems supporting student learning or administrative records (Baepler & Murdoch, 2010; Ferguson, 2012; Romero & Ventura, 2013). Ready access to data enhances its value, allowing for rapid turnaround from data gathering and analysis to utilization. This evolution has expanded the real-time use of information (West, 2012) and vastly increased the value of the work of institutional researchers. At the same time, the rapid growth of ready access data has altered the role of institutional researchers.

The immediate application of these developments had a tremendous influence on the scope of work in IR. It enabled faculty, policymakers, and administrators to capture important components in student-level behaviors and establish possible relationships to the students' academic achievement (such as student persistence, progress in their academic path, and early departure.)

The dynamic information systems and data analysis techniques inspired by data mining evolved from earlier research on knowledge management in higher education dating back to the 1990s. In higher education, data mining is able to zero in on individual student outcomes. This level of detail has greatly enhanced the process of discovering "hidden messages" and patterns within large amounts of data and given considerable leverage to analytical methods used in developing models to predict student outcomes. The introduction of data mining techniques allowed institutional researchers to perform one or more of five types of study categories initially presented by Romero and Ventura (2007) and Baker and Yacef (2009) and further organized by others (Baker et al., 2010; Berland et al., 2014; Peña-Ayala, 2013, 2014; Siemens & Baker, 2012): (a) predictive studies, (b) clustering studies, (c) relationship mining, (d) extraction of data for human subjects, and (e) discovery studies with models.

ILLUSTRATIVE EXAMPLE

An interesting illustration of these new capacities within IR is presented by Knauf, Sakurai, Takada, and Tsuruta (2010). Knauf et al. employed techniques that allowed them to update student-level records throughout their enrollment period in lieu of using a static data set where students' qualities were captured only once. They examined student curriculum planning (specifically in the engineering professions) and evaluated a pathway that optimized student learning and success.

Through the development of a "Dynamic Storyboarding System," they evaluated students' learning processes as well as majors' curricula. They simply compared the course pathways and decision making of students in engineering professions and related them to their academic outcomes. Knauf's initial study was mainly descriptive in nature, but it provided the foundation for a further evaluation of the quality of each student pathway and its potential contribution to student success. In a 2013 study, Tsuruta et al. expanded the analysis to answer two broader questions that carry direct benefit to college planning:

(a) What do the successful students' paths have in common? Specifically, what are the common elements that all students who succeed in completing a demanding major curriculum in engineering have in common in terms of course selection, sequencing, and timing?
(b) What distinguishes the paths of more successful students from those of less successful students [in their college studies]?

In other words, could further analysis determine key variables that allow these students to achieve better outcomes in their academic careers (selection of course combinations, timing of courses during the day, course matching in terms of workload, etc.)?

Tsuruta et al. (2013) provide an interesting illustration of the adaptive changes IR is facing, particularly in terms of computing the mined results. They adapt their analysis in relation both to the educational history of the considered students (so the longer that students are part of a study, the more information is gained about their performance) and to the database, whose data are dynamically updated by the students' study results for the data mining technology (at the cohort level), increasing the accuracy of data mining over time. Their study shows that profiling students dynamically (by taking into account their recent history) is likely to improve risk models' predictive accuracy over time. This change provides additional value to colleges' operations. While previous studies (Bahr, 2010; Hu & McCormick, 2012) used profiling data with little or no updates, this study shows that current technologies allow institutional researchers to continually update the student profile and better understand student dynamics.

RELIANCE ON USERS TO ASK FOR WHAT THEY WANT

A key component of the IR mission is to provide research support to senior executives and both academic and administrative units at the campus level. Institutional researchers have to rely on the data requestors to elaborate their needs, yet these individuals often lack the experience needed to craft research questions or understand the complexity of the information available through robust data mining.

In the ever-changing setting of higher education, training data consumers to elaborate their research needs has become mission critical. Education and training of information producers, users, and consumers is part of IR's common set of duties and functions (Association for Institutional Research, 2017). At the same time, the training required for IR professionals to be effective in educating data users is limited. The challenge for most IR offices is that the training to enter the profession does not equip staff members with extensive teaching skills.

The resulting gap is twofold: Data quality is typically addressed and maintained daily by information system professionals, commonly institutional researchers at colleges. However, Wang and Strong's (1996) classic work has demonstrated that data consumers are usually the ones with a broader data quality conceptualization. Colleges and universities do not have a framework to capture aspects of data quality crucial to data consumers. In a recent analysis, Williams (in Powers & Henderson, 2018) notes a gap in colleges' leadership data culture and training that impacts their ability to communicate their information needs to others. Both data quality and data training gaps contribute to the existing challenges in providing actionable data in higher education discussed in the next section.

CURRENT CHALLENGES IN PROVIDING DATA

IR Positions and Roles in Setting a Data Strategy

The implementation of a data strategy empowers IR to interact with other constituencies at a college, university, and system level in ways that should have been built into data and information systems from the outset. The working environment of institutional researchers has substantially changed since the initiation of the field. However, IR professionals rarely took the time to evaluate their daily data utilization in relation to the overall campus's needs and operational constraints. A data strategy enables IR to foster an environment that supports its need for dynamic, and not only static, information; its role in setting the underlying definition and practices of information storage; and its participation in the development of a common data language for all data consumers on campus.

IR professionals view their role in an institution's data strategy as having four components, as illustrated in Figure 11.1.

In setting a data strategy for an institution, IR needs to assert its roles and responsibilities pertaining to:

1. data ownership;
2. data reporting and knowledge management;
3. data integrity; and
4. training and education for data consumers.

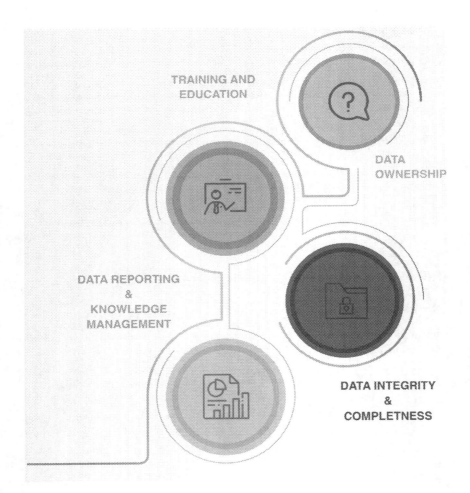

FIGURE 11.1 The Role of IR Professionals in a Data Strategy

Data Ownership

The IR perspective has traditionally been that data are owned by their function area (even when used or reported outside of that area). While many see IR as the exclusive owner of the information, "central data custodian" would be a more accurate description. This role is changing constantly; information access is no longer exclusive to IR function areas (Swing, 2009; Swing & Ross, 2016b), and neither is data ownership. While IR is often responsible for maintaining an institution's official data archives, multiple (and sometimes, competing) data sources may exist within that institution.

The core concepts (or foundations) of data ownership have to be discussed and agreed upon within the institution, and/or the university system. As necessary, the data ownership has to align with local, state, and federal regulations. Specifically, IR needs to address the core elements of data ownership: data access.

Historically, as the primary (or exclusive) data manager, IR provided access to information on an individual or office-to-office basis. There was little thought given to sharing data outside IR or across divisions and applications. Data logic and coding were rarely shared outside the IR office. Changes in technology meant that IR no longer had exclusive control over data. A data strategy must include clear policies that outline the individuals, function titles, and function area(s) that are permitted to access student, campus, and system level data. These policies should also specify the permissions (agreements) for such access, such as read and/or write.

Retention of Information

Among the classic IR functions is the retention of information. A data strategy should specify which information is to be retained and for how long, as well as procedures to destroy electronic information once it is no longer stored or retained, and to securely remove information from hardware, software, and vendor solutions upon completion of their service period. Concurrently, IR needs to take the lead in articulating the proper record level to be maintained (e.g., course level vs. summaries). The cost of electronic data storage is constantly declining, and IR should always favor detailed record level storage over summaries. Detailed student- or campus level records student, or campus level records, allow for constant replication of any higher-order summaries necessary.

Privacy and Security of Data

In its responsibility for retaining information, IR plays a crucial role in securing archival data. A data strategy must go above and beyond the clauses and regulations stipulated in the Family Educational Rights and Privacy Act (FERPA) to address how data users and service providers maintain the security of information. Nissenbaum (2009) notes that the privacy of (student-level) records requires the development of "norms of what information should be used and how within a community." A data strategy should specify policies and mechanisms to secure controlled access to information. Specifically, it should address the level(s) of privacy needed for the protection, use, and sharing of information about individuals (students and staff) in the context of IR.

In addition, a data strategy should state the underlying principles for data storage locations (hardware, software, and cloud solutions), routine data management and maintenance, and the data/disaster recovery plan (DRP). While DRPs are typically developed by the information technology or networking area, it is mission critical that IR take a role in setting the priorities for data recovery, redundancy, and retention of auditable reporting data.

Data Reporting and Knowledge Management

For the majority of colleges and universities, IR is both responsible and accountable for the legal burden of reporting information required under several laws and regulations (Beaudin, 2017; Flood & Roberts, 2017). As a result, IR often leads data governance initiatives on campus. Such policies should address case-specific elements associated with the reporting (e.g., common definitions, data accuracy, reporting standards, and timelines). Because the modern working environment of campuses involves an ever-growing awareness of information, IR must set guidelines, rules, and mechanisms to ensure that knowledge management is based on uniform data usage and definitions. Furthermore, IR must establish clear rules for archiving all information in a readily accessible format (both reports and data sources).

As noted earlier, IR advocates storing detail-level information whenever possible, as this allows for aggregation in any applicable summaries. At the same time, IR needs to take charge of organizing institutional knowledge. While reporting draws upon existing information systems, IR is responsible for serving as the institutional knowledge manager. An integrated IR data strategy includes not only gathering raw data and transforming it into useful information for college operations but also promoting a consistent approach to identifying, capturing, evaluating, retrieving, and sharing campus- and system-based information assets. Knowledge may be gathered from documents, policies, and procedures but IR needs to develop mechanisms for storing, indexing, and sharing that knowledge, which may include information on particular students or campus practices that will support continual student success.

While IR has been involved in managing knowledge for nearly 20 years, there is an ever-growing need to develop knowledge management techniques that fit the modern IR environment.

Data Integrity

From the IR perspective, data integrity addresses three dimensions of the information stored in administrative records: consistency, accuracy, and completeness. Final and archival information should remain unchanged across multiple queries or instances of a record. Current, dynamic, and non-finalized information may change within the business rules associated with the data.

To ensure data integrity, a process involving checks and balances must be established and clearly followed. This process should include various stages for data checking and verification, e.g., matching the transaction-level records to the totals in specific categories, constantly examining the records to ensure that all values in the fields are valid (and applicable), and generating regular error reports. Institutional researchers who work with the information regularly can inform the process as they evaluate the values not only for database field definitions but also for content. IR can set a rule to examine values that may seem valid but do not fit the settings of the institution (e.g., a valid degree program prior to the establishment of such a program at an institution). Involving IR in the creation of a data integrity plan ensures that the plan will account for the specific context of the institution and enhances data quality.

It is advantageous to include IR in the process of testing dynamic (non-finalized) information for integrity. Due to its unique position, IR is often in charge of providing current information for regulatory or grant operation purposes. Leaving IR out of a data strategy conversation may hinder an institution's ability to address requests for information crucial to its operations. Furthermore, collaborating with IR ensures that the conversion of dynamic data into census ("frozen") data will take place without interruption to any required reporting and that all data sources align properly.

Training and Education for Data Consumers

In the ever-changing information environment, training data consumers has become mission critical for IR. The challenge for most institutional researchers is that their professional background has not adequately equipped them to accomplish this goal.

In order to master the multiple means of data manipulation and analysis in higher education, data consumers need training not only in the technology but also in the policy, behavioral, and ethical aspects of a large administrative records repository within the higher education context. First, the increase in data access requires IR to take a greater role in the adoption of standards-, content-, and compliance-oriented training for studies involving human subjects. The existing data strategies do not emphasize that both current and archival records are protected under Institutional Review Board (IRB) policies. Institutional researchers now face the need to educate users not only with regard to the data analysis but also with regard to adapting the analysis to accommodate human subject protection rules.

Second, the growth of big data has created a need for IR not only to provide human subject protection training but also to address student record privacy concerns. For example, the exponential growth of dynamic dashboards and readily available data interfaces has not aligned with training and technological solutions that limit that access to identifiable records. IR needs to help develop training to ensure records privacy, an ever-growing concern among parents, students, and college administrators. Vendors and developers must be educated to evaluate and test data accessibility not only for reporting purposes but also for data protection.

Third, institutional researchers are required to explain the limits of the variable definitions in existing databases and educate users with regard both to the content of the information and to any limitations on analysis. In other words, involving IR is essential to ensure that data are used within its context and in line with its methodological limits. The recent changes in college and university settings require IR professionals to educate both themselves and their institutions in a wide range of issues relating to compliance and research ethics, as well as to provide statistical, research, and analytical training to data consumers.

WHAT WE REALLY WANT USERS TO UNDERSTAND

Developing and implementing successful data strategy requires the collaboration of all applicable units at the institutional and system level. It is crucial to ensure that institutional researchers will not be a stand-alone, isolated data reporting unit. In order for colleges and universities to utilize the powerful information available to them, they must integrate IR into the decision making process at all levels.

In the daily operations of IR offices, reporting requirements weigh heavily on staff. Institutions should seek to better manage this workload and increase the direct contribution of IR to student and college-level success. The changing environment of higher education has expanded the number and variety of campus level decision makers who need to access information; along with administrators, students and faculty now require access to data and training in how to use it. A data strategy should take all those groups into account, in particular by evaluating how best to meet their educational and training needs both today and in the future.

> **DISCUSSION QUESTIONS**
>
> 1. How can IR find a balance between making data accessible to a broad audience and fulfilling its responsibility to safeguard the security of that data?
> 2. Considering the increased the number of units and individuals with direct access to data, how should IR address growing concerns on campus about data integrity?
> 3. Can a single training program address the needs of all data consumers in a campus setting? What are the core aspects of data education and training that must be available universally?
> 4. How does one ensure that the technological developments in IR data will not lead to "data fishing" in lieu of promoting student and campus success?
> 5. What would be the most efficient ways to promote coordination between IR and IT? In many colleges and universities, these two function areas are isolated and require complex coordination. Institutions should consider integrating IT and IR for greater efficiency.

REFERENCES

Association for Institutional Research. (2017). *Duties and Functions of Institutional Research*. Retrieved from www.airweb.org/docs/default-source/documents-for-pages/air-duties-and-functions-of_ire96e442e8924495cb1f954be7c9012ca.pdf

Baepler, P., & Murdoch, C. J. (2010). Academic analytics and data mining in higher education. *International Journal for the Scholarship of Teaching and Learning*, 4(2), 17.

Bahr, P. R. (2010). The bird's eye view of community colleges: A behavioral typology of first-time students based on cluster analytic classification. *Research in Higher Education*, 51(8), 724–749.

Baker, R. S., Pechenizkiy, M., Romero, C., & Ventura, S. (2010). *Handbook of Educational Data Mining*. New York: CRC Press.

Baker, R. S., & Yacef, K. (2009). The state of educational data mining in 2009: A review and future visions. *JEDM-Journal of Educational Data Mining, 1*(1), 3–17.

Beaudin, K. (2017). The legal implications of storing student data: Preparing for and responding to data breaches. *New Directions for Institutional Research, 2016*(172), 37–48. doi:10.1002/ir.20202

Berland, M., Baker, R. S., & Blikstein, P. (2014). Educational data mining and learning analytics: Applications to constructionist research. *Technology, Knowledge and Learning, 19*(1–2), 205–220.

Ferguson, R. (2012). Learning analytics: Drivers, developments and challenges. *International Journal of Technology Enhanced Learning, 4*(5), 304–317.

Flood, J. T., & Roberts, J. (2017). the evolving nature of higher education accreditation: Legal considerations for institutional research leaders. *New Directions for Institutional Research, 172*, 73–84. doi:10.1002/ir.20205

Heiner, C., Heffernan, N., & Barnes, T. (2007). Educational data mining. Paper presented at the Supplementary Proceedings of the 12th International Conference of Artificial Intelligence in Education.

Hu, S., & McCormick, A. (2012). An engagement-based student typology and its relationship to college outcomes. *Research in Higher Education, 53*(7), 738–754. doi:10.1007/s11162-012-9254-7

Junco, R., & Cotten, S. R. (2011). Perceived academic effects of instant messaging use. *Computers & Education, 56*(2), 370–378. doi:10.1016/j.compedu.2010.08.020

Knauf, R., Sakurai, Y., Takada, K., & Tsuruta, S. (2010). Validation of a data mining method for optimal university curricula. Paper presented at the International Workshop on Design, Evaluation and Refinement of Intelligent Systems (DERIS2010).

Luan, J. (2002). Data mining and its applications in higher education. *New Directions for Institutional Research, 113*, 17–36.

Luan, J. (2007). Data mining applications in higher education: Executive report SPSS. Retrieved from www.pse.pt/Documentos/Data%20mining%20in%20higher%20education.pdf

Nissenbaum, H. (2009). *Privacy in Context: Technology, Policy, and the Integrity of Social Life.* Stanford, CA: Stanford University Press.

Peña-Ayala, A. (2013). *Intelligent and Adaptive Educational-Learning Systems: Achievements and Trends.* New York, Dordrecht, London: Springer.

Peña-Ayala, A. (2014). Educational data mining: A survey and a data mining-based analysis of recent works. *Expert Systems with Applications, 41*(4), 1432–1462.

Powers, K., & Henderson, A. E. (2018). *Cultivating a Data Culture in Higher Education.* New York: Routledge.

Romero, C., & Ventura, S. (2007). Educational data mining: A survey from 1995 to 2005. *Expert Systems with Applications, 33*(1), 135–146.

Romero, C., & Ventura, S. (2010). Educational data mining: A review of the state of the art. *Systems, Man, and Cybernetics, Part C: Applications and Reviews, IEEE Transactions On, 40*(6), 601–618.

Romero, C., & Ventura, S. (2013). Data mining in education. *Wiley Interdisciplinary Reviews: Data Mining and Knowledge Discovery, 3*(1), 12–27.

Serban, A. M. (2002). Knowledge management: The "fifth face" of institutional research. *New Directions for Institutional Research, 2002*(113), 105–112. doi:10.1002/ir.40

Siemens, G., & Baker, R. S. (2012). Learning analytics and educational data mining: Towards communication and collaboration. Paper presented at the Proceedings of the 2nd International Conference on Learning Analytics and Knowledge.

Swing, R. L. (2009). Institutional researchers as change agents. *New Directions for Institutional Research, 2009*(143), 5–16. doi:10.1002/ir.301

Swing, R. L., & Ross, L. E. (2016a). A new vision for institutional research. *Change: the Magazine of Higher Learning, 48*(2), 6–13. doi:10.1080/00091383.2016.1163132

Swing, R. L., & Ross, L. E. (2016b). Statement of aspirational practice for institutional research. Tallahassee, FL: Association for Institutional Research. Accessed October, 15, 2017.

Tsuruta, S., Knauf, R., Dohi, S., Kawabe, T., & Sakurai, Y. (2013). An intelligent system for modeling and supporting academic educational processes. In A. Peña-Ayala (Ed.), *Intelligent and Adaptive Educational-Learning Systems* (Vol 17, pp. 469–496). Berlin, Heidelberg: Springer.

Volkwein, J. F. (1999). The four faces of institutional research. *New Directions for Institutional Research, 1999*(104), 9–19.

Wang, R. Y., & Strong, D. M. (1996). Beyond accuracy: What data quality means to data consumers. *Journal of Management Information Systems, 12*(4), 5–33.

Webber, K. L. (2018). *Building Capacity in Institutional Research and Decision Support in Higher Education*. (Vol 4). Berlin, Heidelberg: Springer.

West, D. M. (2012). Big data for education: Data mining, data analytics, and web dashboards. *Governance Studies at Brookings*, 1–10.

Chapter 12

Information Technology Analysts' Perspectives

Derek MacPherson

INTRODUCTION

In the context of building a data strategy, an information technology (IT) analyst is a data analyst that works for the information technology department or a similar IT unit, such as data management or business intelligence. In a higher education environment, this individual's goal is to provide timely and actionable data, information, and analysis to facilitate student success and institutional growth. A timely deliverable is one that is ready when the user or requester needs it. For instance, if an institutional research analyst requests raw detail data to complete a regulatory report, they should receive it early enough to allow them to file the regulatory report before the deadline.

By "actionable," we mean that the intended recipient is able to act based on the deliverable. For example, a college or university might use attendance or grade data to identify students who would benefit from interventions before they fail a class or withdraw from the institution. Data that arrives too late or are too ambiguous to act upon are ineffective, and are not consistent with a data strategy.

As institutions develop a data strategy, it seems logical to involve the professionals who know the most about where the data rests in data systems. Accordingly, this chapter begins with a description of an IT analyst, before describing the role's involvement in activities that connect to a data strategy, such as working with the multiple data strategy stakeholders. The chapter concludes with sections on difficult components of the position, current challenges in providing data, and what IT analysts really want users to understand.

INFORMATION TECHNOLOGY ANALYSTS' PERSPECTIVES

DESCRIPTION OF AN IT ANALYST

An IT analyst generally provides three basic types of deliverables. The first is detail level data, such as non-aggregated student, enrollment, course, or transaction-level data. In this case, the requester would be another analyst, perhaps an institutional research analyst or data scientist, doing their own statistical modeling, research, synthesis, or analysis. Depending on how the institution's data systems are organized, the IT analyst might have access to a broader range of source data.

Alternatively, the IT analyst might be able to facilitate a data collection mechanism in a data warehouse or other information system. A data warehouse is a central repository for data from across the entity. Figure 12.1 is a generic example of a data warehouse supporting an academic institution. Organizations typically consolidate current and historical data from multiple applications or data systems into a data warehouse to support institutional data analysis and managerial decision making.

The second type of deliverable is aggregated data, or what some refer to as information (as opposed to data). This is summarized data and falls between raw detail–level data and analysis. The target audience for this type of deliverable is frequently senior leadership; such information is also required for external reporting. In these cases, the recipients are more interested in a summarized or executive-level view than in raw or detail data.

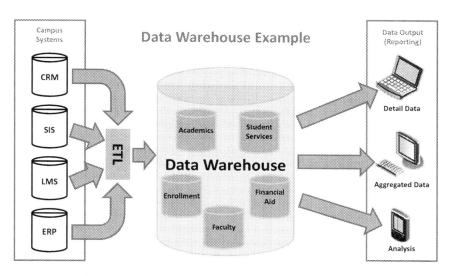

FIGURE 12.1 Generic Example of a Data Warehouse Supporting an Academic Institution

169

The third type of deliverable is analysis. Depending on the higher education institution's size, it will often have many individuals doing their own analysis, of which the IT analyst might be just one. However, since not all leaders will have their own staff analyst, the IT analyst can examine and interpret data as necessary. In addition, a smaller institution may want to centralize its data analysts, either in its IT or business intelligence department, for efficiency. Finally, the IT analyst is often the best person to take a one-time or ad hoc analysis, whether their own or someone else's, and operationalize it into a reoccurring reporting channel for the institution.

Ultimately, any IT department or analyst exists to serve the greater institution and its goals, which revolve around student success. The IT analyst can assist in identifying and providing key performance metrics. Take student onboarding, for example. An IT analyst can use data to measure how fast incoming transcripts are evaluated and financial aid is processed, or characteristics of students who withdraw from the institution.

IT ANALYST ACTIVITIES THAT CONNECT TO A DATA STRATEGY

Working with Multiple Stakeholders

IT analysts see themselves as data analysts and feel that they play a central role in facilitating an institution-wide data culture. The above described provide detailed, aggregated, and analyzed data to support institutional requirements related to external reporting, internal analysis, decision making, and ongoing operational processes. The IT analyst thus supports key members of the institution. Who the user or requester is determines the level or type of data the IT analyst furnishes. The president and vice presidents usually require either highly aggregated or analyzed data, as senior leaders have little time to examine un-aggregated or under-aggregated detail data. This type of reporting supports strategic-level internal analysis and decision making.

Developing Key Reports for Stakeholders

In contrast to the strategic-level reporting prepared for senior leaders, faculty needs more operational reporting, which the IT analyst furnishes as detail and aggregated data. Detail level reporting can assist faculty members by providing section-level and student-level detail data to identify academic success and opportunities for improvement, such as measuring learning outcomes. In addition, the analyst can aggregate detail data from grades, course drop rates, end-of-course student surveys, and other sources to provide performance metrics for faculty and departments. While many academic systems incorporate basic reporting, some users may require more customized solutions; data from multiple systems combined into one report; or a report delivery method not natively supported by the application, such as email or texting.

Separate from the faculty and academic departments are the individual departments that make up the administration of the institution, such as student affairs, the registrar, financial aid, finance and student accounts, admissions, and legal and external affairs. IT analysts provide the non-academic departments and units with a combination of aggregated and detail data. Frequently, the aggregated reporting supports operational requirements, such as the accounting department's month-end closing or end-of-quarter reporting. Aggregated data can also serve to assess the overall performance of departments, units, teams, or even individuals. Similarly, members of non-academic departments can use detail data for day-to-day operational processing, exception identification, and even validation of the aggregated reporting.

Working with Institutional Research

In addition to senior leadership, academic and non-academic departments, and faculty, one of the most important groups that IT analysts can support is the institutional research team. While typically small in number, institutional research analysts have a high degree of analytical ability and institutional knowledge. They are also more than qualified to aggregate and summarize detail data. However, they may lack access to the disparate data systems across the institution, or the tools needed to extract that data in a usable form. In such cases, the IT analyst can furnish the needed detail data.

IT Data Positions

As described above, IT analysts provide data to different types of users across the institution, and are undoubtedly integral to developing a data culture. However, since IT analysts are really data or reporting analysts, they do not stand alone to support the institution on their own. Instead, they head an unseen supporting cast that can be quite large, depending on the size of the overall organization.

First in line are database administrators (DBAs), who are ultimately responsible for maintaining the databases in a way that both preserves the integrity of the data and makes the data available to appropriate users, applications, and systems. If the institution has an internally supported data warehouse, then there is likely a suite of other essential data positions, the number of which depends on the size of the institution and the amount of dedicated resources. As shown in Table 12.1, these might include a project

Table 12.1 Frequent IT Data Positions

Position or Role	Role Definition
Business Analyst	Works with institutional or business stakeholder to develop document requirements. Is typically an expert in the subject matter and interprets non-technical requests and descriptions into technical requirements.
Change Management/ Compliance Specialist	Ensures all IT changes that may materially impact the institution comply with internal controls. Intended to prevent improperly tested software changes from being implemented and negatively impacting the institution.
Data Governance Analyst	Works with institutional stakeholders to ensure that high data quality exists throughout the lifecycle of the data. Frequently develops a set of terms to describe the data, which is then used across the organization.
Database Administrator (DBA)	Maintains the availability of the databases and data systems.
Data Warehouse/Software/ ETL/BI Developer	Creates and maintains software that populates the data warehouse from multiple source systems into one consolidated location.
IT/Data/Reporting Analyst	Develops ad hoc and recurring detail, aggregated, and analytical reports.
Ops/DevOps Engineer	Monitors and troubleshoots IT processes.
Product Manager	Typically manages a single software application's life cycle, including the collection of initial requirements, software development, midlife updates and maintenance, and decommissioning.
Project Manager	Manages a particular software project or implementation with defined start and end points. Can be across products, platforms, or particular software applications.
Quality Assurance (QA) Analyst	Performance testing to ensure that any software, hardware, or configuration changes meet the organization's requirements and do not cause unintended changes to existing systems.
Requester/End User	Members of the organization requesting data or analysis, typically outside the IT, BI, or DM departments.

or product manager to coordinate; a business analyst to define requirements; data warehouse developers to write the software; quality assurance (QA) analysts to ensure that requirements are met; and possibly change management, internal audit, or compliance personnel to document that proper controls were applied to the development and deployment process.

Smaller institutions can consolidate two or more of the above positions into one, and may not need some roles at all. However, the larger the institution, the more important it is that each role be filled by a different, qualified individual with a specialized skill set, for three mutually reinforcing reasons. First, the scope, scale, and complexity of the requisite work increases in proportion with the institution's size. Second, individuals with highly specialized skill sets may not be adequately equipped or qualified to fill other roles. Finally, maintaining roles separate makes replacing any one individual less disruptive and prevents conflicts of interest (such as data warehouse developers validating or QA'ing their own work), thus mitigating overall risk to the institution.

DIFFICULT COMPONENTS OF THE POSITION

There are six important components of being an effective IT analyst at a college or university.

Knowledge of Relational Databases

The first is a knowledge of relational databases, campus-specific systems, and institutional policies. As most applications and systems found at an institution of higher education store data in relational databases, it is important for an IT analyst to understand the principles of the relational data model and the programming language used to extract data from databases, SQL. While there are software packages that can enable end users with limited knowledge of databases to create reports and dashboards by themselves, these tools usually require an IT analyst or equivalent to configure or populate them with data.

In addition to understanding databases, IT analysts also need to understand campus-specific applications that generate data. Frequently, schools will have multiple systems that may or may not be integrated. For example, an institution may use both a student information system (SIS) to manage student records and a learning management system (LMS) to allow faculty to deliver instruction, either in part or in full. While these two systems may be dependent on each other, their respective data may not be fully integrated from a reporting standpoint. In such a scenario, understanding how the SIS and LMS relate would facilitate timely and accurate reporting.

After databases and campus-specific applications, the final piece of knowledge that IT analysts require in order to maximize their effectiveness is an understanding of institutional policies. Any increase in the size of the student body and/or the number of programs offered has a direct impact on the complexity of these policies. This policy complexity in turn impacts data interaction and aggregation, and consequently reporting and analysis. Thus, it would behoove an IT analyst in a higher education environment to learn as much as possible about the institution's policies.

Interacting with Non-Technical Faculty and Staff

Second, an IT analyst needs the ability to interact with non-technical faculty and staff. This can be both crucial and challenging, since IT professionals frequently immerse themselves in technical details and jargon, while many faculty and staff members' expertise lies outside the technical realm. Table 12.2 lists some common IT terms that may be unfamiliar to most users. The IT analyst must therefore convert non-technical requests and descriptions into technical requirements, unless the institution and the specific project are large enough to warrant a business analyst who can assist in that regard.

As part of the "translation" process, the IT analyst needs to be able to explain technical definitions, constraints, and limitations of the source data to non–technically inclined faculty and staff. One limitation might be that the institution's current systems do not collect a particular piece of data. Similarly, the systems might retain only the current value for a requested piece of data, and not the historical value or the change history. In some cases, a good analyst will be able to suggest proxies for the non-retained data, at least looking backward. They may also be able to recommend changes that will allow the institution's applications or data systems to collect and store that information going forward, such as in a data warehouse.

Skilled in Using Technical Tools

Third, an IT analyst must be skilled in using the technical tools available at that institution, or tools the institution is willing to acquire. These usually include a data extraction or manipulation language, as well as some type of reporting software. Data languages are typically a proprietary version of SQL (meaning each software vendor has its own unique version). For reporting tools, IT analysts use a combination of Microsoft Excel, Power BI, Tableau, Crystal Reports, and Microsoft Access. Some database vendors provide their own native reporting tools, such as Microsoft's SQL Server Reporting Services (SSRS) or Oracle's Discoverer, Reports, or OBIEE. In any case, an analyst needs a method of querying the data from the applications or underlying data structures and then a way of formatting their results into a usable report.

Table 12.2 Terms Commonly Used by IT Analysts

Terms Commonly Used by IT Analysts

Term	Abbreviation	Definition
Business Intelligence	BI	Strategies and technologies used to analyze data, and ideally provide current, historical, and predictive information.
Customer-Relationship Management	CRM	Software used by institutions to centralize and manage data on its interactions with current and potential students.
Data Management	DM	Process of collecting, processing, storing, and making data available to the appropriate users.
Data Mart		A subset of the data warehouse focused on a single line of business, department, team, or other area of interest.
Data Warehouse	DW	An enterprise-wide central repository for current and historical data integrated from one or more disparate sources. Potentially allows analyst to report from a single location.
Extract Translate Load	ETL	A process whereby data is extracted out of a source system, translated, and then loaded into another system. Frequently associated with data warehousing.
Learning Management System	LMS	A software application used by educational institutions to deliver, document, and report educational courses.
Relational Database Management System	RDBMS	The most common form of database and thus the basis of most data applications.
Sequential Query Language	SQL	The standard database programming language, used to process and extract data from structure. Pronounced "sequel."
Student Information System	SIS	An application used by educational institutions to manage student records, such as admissions, enrollments, grades, transcripts, and financial aid.
Quality Assurance	QA	Validating the software development process to ensure quality and limit disruptions to the institution due to detectable errors.

Analytical Ability

Fourth, ideally, an IT analyst has analytical ability. While analytical ability is obviously essential for data analysis, it is also important for reporting even detailed or aggregated data when working with diverse data sources. However, the best IT analysts may not have traditional IT backgrounds or degrees in IT intensive subjects such as computer science or software engineering, but will come instead from a variety of backgrounds. One is social science, particularly with exposure to statistics and quantitative methodologies. Another background typical of successful IT analysts is accounting, where compiling, reporting, and interpreting detailed and aggregated data are a key skillset. These types of backgrounds are particular helpful in understand and analyzing institutional data.

Anticipate Follow-Up Questions

Fifth, an experienced, high-performing IT analyst should be able to anticipate likely follow-up questions. This is especially true if the analyst is working with familiar requesters. For example, after aggregating the data per the initial requirements, a good analyst will step back and try to interpret the results. Based on that interpretation, they can come up with likely follow-up questions, which they can then answer by using or modifying the existing data set to provide the necessary level of aggregation or analysis.

Overcome Significant Challenges by Finding Creative Solutions

Sixth, an IT analyst must overcome significant challenges, such as data and data system limitations, data silos, and data turf. Data systems may not retain all the relevant data, or diverse data systems may not easily tie to each other; for instance, it may be difficult to link initial admission inquiries to specific students or specific courses of enrollment. Different departments, colleges, or institutional initiatives may create their own independent data systems that are not tied to the data systems employed by the institution as a whole, and may be unknown outside a small group of users. A corollary of that is the "I want your data, but you can't see mine" syndrome, where one group has sought-after data that they refuse to share, all the while expecting other groups to share data with them. Of course, even when such restrictions are appropriate, this type of scenario undermines the development of a broader data culture.

Reliance on Users to Ask for What They Want

Ultimately, IT analysts and their immediate department, whether it be information technology, data management, or business intelligence, are tasked with providing actionable information to serve the needs of the institution. Their priorities therefore tend to be set by the institution as a whole and by (or at least through) individual requesters, rather than by the data department per se. Although IT analysts can develop informed opinions and provide suggestions as to what reporting or analysis would be helpful, they are not charged with running the institution or any department or college within it, and thus may not be in the best position to determine requirements.

Articulating the Data Request

Given the above, an IT analyst may find it ironic that requesters, end users, and institution members frequently have trouble defining what they want or need. On closer inspection, however, this situation is entirely understandable for several reasons. First, requesters may be uncertain about what data they need until they see it. For example, a requester may be aware of a gap in reporting or is attempting to address a perceived operational shortcoming. They may have one or more theories as to the cause of the shortcoming but obviously need supporting data. These types of cases frequently evolve into iterative exploratory projects, with multiple rounds of data collection and report building, and the requester evaluating each set of results.

Multiple Data Sources

A second reason requesters may face challenges in defining their needs is that they are not always aware of all potential sources of data. Institutions frequently have multiple applications and data systems, and faculty and staff members may only be familiar with those they use. The requester may effectively be working in a data silo. Ideally, the IT analyst should have a broader understanding of the available sources of data and thus be able to help mitigate this shortfall.

Institutional Policies Influence How the Data are Pulled

Yet another reason requesters struggle with articulating their requirements is that even if they are aware of all the potential sources of data, they may not be familiar with all of the associated institutional policies. An experienced IT analyst at a higher learning institution will have built up networks of people to ask. The analyst may also have worked on a similar project that exposed them to the policies in question. An effective data governance program at the institution could incorporate relevant policies in the enterprise-wide data definitions.

Data Requests to Confirm Existing Beliefs

A final factor that can undermine a requester's ability to provide clear requirements is confirmation bias, defined as "the seeking or interpreting of evidence in ways that are partial to existing beliefs, expectations, or a hypothesis in hand" (Nickerson, 1998, p. 175). In this case, the individual is only requesting data either to confirm what they already think they know or to support a current position, potentially overlooking other data sources and reporting solutions.

CURRENT CHALLENGES IN PROVIDING DATA

Centralized vs Decentralized Data Experts

IT analysts can encounter a litany of other challenges in providing data, some of which result from the decentralized nature of many institutions of higher education. Decentralized organizations lead to "silos of excellence", duplication of effort, and insufficiently integrated data systems. In management circles around the year 2000, the "center of excellence" (COE) concept began to increase in popularity across numerous industries. A COE is an entity that concentrates leaders and specialists in a particular area, skill set, or expertise with the expectation that the resulting synergy will disproportionally increase the group's qualitative and quantitative production for the larger organization.

However, in larger organizations as well as those that are geographically distributed or have disbursed centers of power (departments or colleges that act autonomously), new "reporting shops" proliferate. That is, each semi-autonomous entity creates its own data reporting or analysis group to meet its own needs, particularly when central IT is unable to meet those needs in a timely manner. These groups could be termed "silos of excellence" because while they may perform competent analysis with an expertise in a very narrow field, they often work independently of others doing the same tasks elsewhere in the institution, with all the advantages and disadvantages that that entails.

Unintended Consequences of Decentralization

Once a number of silos of excellence exist, several phenomena tend to occur. One is that individual requesters shop around for the group that will complete the request the fastest, provide the most favorable data or analysis to support their current position, or both. In this scenario, one requester submits the same request to one or more groups, creating duplication of effort and reducing the total output of the organization.

Another silo of excellence phenomenon is when several departments or colleges encounter a similar data or reporting challenge and each submits a request through a different channel. This results in several different analysts working nearly identical data or analysis requests in isolation, likely producing outcomes that slightly favor one department or college over another. From an IT analyst's perspective, both phenomena—one requester making the same request multiple times or multiple requesters making similar requests—create frustrating inefficiencies, consume valuable resources, and inhibit completion of other unrelated requests.

Along with duplication of effort and silos of excellence, insufficiently integrated data systems represent another challenge of decentralized organizations. In one potential scenario, a semi-autonomous department or college might create or implement a new data system, such as a pilot program, without sufficiently discussing the technical requirements, timing of the event, or other essential details with all the relevant entities within the larger organization. Regardless of how the disparate systems originate, their mere existence creates reporting and data challenges. Common data points between systems are not as prolific as one might hope. One way that organizations with successful data cultures deal with disparate systems is by consolidating all data in a data warehouse.

Another major challenge in providing data is when demand for data, reporting, and analysis outstrips supply. In general, a data-driven culture encourages users throughout the institution to think of new ways to use data. This naturally increases the demand for data, taxing the resources of the IT department. A common result is the creation of new reporting teams and further decentralization, with all the associated challenges of decentralization.

Differing Data Definitions

A related challenge is that the definitions of terms used to describe data elements may vary from group to group. When data reporting functions become unstructured and decentralized, the natural tendency is for each reporting or data entity to create its own set of terms or term definitions. One example of conflicting definitions is where single terms have multiple definitions, depending on which group originates the reporting. This might not be a problem if the resulting data reports remain within the entity that created them. However, reports that have conflicting term definitions seem to propagate throughout institutions. When leadership compares two such reports, both sets of results might be accurate, but the different definitions can suggest that they conflict, discrediting both reports and creating confusion. A similarly confusing situation occurs when multiple terms have the same definition. Either way, the end result is conflicting data and distrust in the data and reporting.

Typically, organizations address these types of term definition challenges in one of two ways. One method is to centralize reporting in one entity or department, which can then impose uniform definitions. This is effective only in hierarchical, top-down organizations with a level of control that can prohibit the proliferation of new reporting groups. A more standard methodology frequently found in organizations that have a strong data culture is to set up a program to "govern" the terms used in data reporting. A successful data governance program involves the continued commitment of key stakeholders, who must first meet regularly to decide on term definitions and then adhere to the agreed-upon definitions. The disadvantage of a governance program is that it requires a high degree of support from across the institution. Without widespread buy-in, the two required steps—establishment of and adherence to definitions—are unlikely to take place.

Integrated Data Systems

Another major challenge is that institutions' data systems are not always sufficiently integrated. Insufficient integration creates data silos, inhibiting the kind of data fusion that can provide true, original insights. In some cases, the user and the analyst are unaware of all the data that could be available to them. Yet even when the IT analyst is aware of the data, unintegrated data systems will slow their ability to fulfill the user's request. This slowness is because they are forced to use ad hoc or inefficient techniques, such as manually exporting text, importing large amounts of data, or joining the multiple data sets on problematic columns that produce false matches, such as names or email addresses. Of course, the traditional permanent solution for countering data integration challenges is to develop an institutional data warehouse, but this requires a significant ongoing investment of time and resources.

Cognitive Biases

Still another major challenge is the cognitive bias of both the requester and the provider of the data. The first type of cognitive bias is a self-serving bias, a term that describes the tendency to perceive oneself or one's organization in an overly favorable manner that may distort the normal cognitive processes (Kruglanski & Higgins, 2007). In a data-requesting context, this means that the request requirements and the term definitions used have an inherent bias in favor of the requester or requesting entity. The requester consciously or unconsciously wants to validate their group's performance or to measure only the metrics that their group most values. In many ways, this is similar to the term definition issue, except in this case the requester or reporting entity defines terms in a way that has a favorable bias.

The second type of cognitive bias is confirmation bias, which typically "connotes the seeking or interpreting of evidence in ways that are partial to existing beliefs, expectations, or a hypothesis in hand" (Nickerson, 1998). In this instance, the requester has a theory, which is possibly favorable to them, and is searching for supporting data. The potential liability of the confirmation bias—and that which makes it anathema to a data culture—is that it leads to ignoring or overlooking evidence that undermines the preferred theory or supports an alternative theory.

Incorporating New and Emerging Technologies

The final major challenge in providing data are incorporating new and emerging technologies. These can generate valuable information but are also associated with increased risk as they can be time and resource consuming and may not produce the desired outcome. Techniques in the emerging field of predictive analytics include using predictive analytics, such as using predictive modeling on current and historical data to identify patterns and calculate the probability of likely future outcomes. A subset of predictive analytics is machine learning, a technique associated with artificial intelligence where induction and other types of algorithms use statistical data to allow the computer or program to "learn" without explicit programming.

WHAT IT ANALYSTS REALLY WANT USERS TO UNDERSTAND

From an IT analyst's perspective, there are a couple of key takeaways for users and data consumers.

Clear Data Requests

First, as much as reasonably possible, thoroughly think through the data or analysis requirements before submitting a request. For example, in a new data or analysis request that utilizes existing data, an IT analyst would prefer that the requester assiduously define each required data element, leveraging or adhering to data-governed definitions when possible. While institutional data can be ambiguous or opaque, IT analysts tend to be very literal, prefer a black and white world, and frown on any shades of gray in the data, data definitions, or request requirements.

A user can safely assume that if a requirement can be interpreted in more than one way, the IT analyst will inadvertently choose the way most antithetical to the user's intention. This outcome leads to incorrectly interpreted or reported data, the IT analyst redoing their work, or both. Unsurprisingly, neither the user nor the analyst is happy. The user may feel that they did not receive what they requested. The IT analyst's perspective is that they may not have delivered what was wanted, but they did deliver what was requested.

A more reasonable perspective for both user and analyst is to expect an iterative development process, depending on requirements and data availability. In this context, "iterative" means multiple rounds of development by the IT analyst, draft reports submitted to the requester, feedback from the requester to the IT analyst, and then further development by the IT analyst.

Data Reporting from New Systems

Along with providing clear requirements for requests that involve existing data, users should carefully consider likely future reporting requirements before implementing new systems, processes, or even pilot projects. When an institution implements a new data system, either developed in-house or acquired from an external party, the developers may have envisioned one set of reporting requirements. After the implementation, institutional users of the new system may become aware of reporting gaps that they had not previously anticipated. Such epiphanies can result in unexpected, accelerated, and potentially unwelcome development projects for the IT analyst.

Context and Detail Can Save Time and Frustration for All

When IT analysts ask users and requesters to explain requests clearly, they usually mean two things. First, provide the IT analyst the big picture by describing both the background of the request and the ultimate goal of the project. For background, it can be helpful to the analyst to hear the origins of the need and the level of urgency. For the goal, describe the desired end state for the request, how the request will solve the original problem, and how the institution will benefit from the successful completion of the request. This context can be of enormous help when the IT analyst is interpreting requirements and definitions, or encounters muddled or unexpected data.

Second, provide IT analyst the most granular requirement details known to the requester, including data examples when applicable. For instance, provide student-level examples, possibly with screen shots of the front-end system. IT analysts really just want users and requesters to be as specific as possible with the requirement details about the data they desire. Sharing both the big picture and the nuanced details with the IT analyst fosters good communication. Likewise, open communication lines between users and analysts can enhance working relationships and contribute to developing a positive data culture.

DISCUSSION QUESTIONS

1. Of the three types of data deliverables typically provided by an IT analyst, which do you perceive your institution values the most? Which is the most requested?
2. Describe how a data governance process might work at your institution. What would be the largest obstacles to a data governance program? What would the key benefits of data governance be to your institution?
3. What types of cognitive bias are the most common in data requests in a higher education environment?
4. Grade the integration level of your institution's applications and data systems. In what ways could your institution improve the integration of its systems?
5. One of the largest challenges for any IT analyst is ambiguous or ill-defined terms. What are three ways that users at your institution can best mitigate these types of challenges?

REFERENCES

Kruglanski, A. W., & Higgins, E. T. (2007). *Social Psychology: Handbook of Basic Principles.* New York: Guilford Press. Retrieved from http://search.ebscohost.com/login aspx?direct=true&db=cat02191a&AN=aul.10201017&site=eds-live&scope=site

Nickerson, R. S. (1998). Confirmation bias: A ubiquitous phenonmenon in many guises. *Review of General Psychology, 2*(2), 175–220.

Biographies

BOOK EDITOR

Kristina Powers, PhD is President of the Institute for Effectiveness in Higher Education. Kristina also serves as a national IPEDS (Integrated Postsecondary Education Data System) trainer and a Research Fellow on Student Achievement with the WASC Senior College and University Commission (WSCUC). She has headed institutional research, institutional effectiveness, and assessment offices as well as served as accreditation liaison at multiple public, private not-for-profit, and private for-profit institutions. Other higher education roles have included lead author for the *Statements of Aspirational Practice for Institutional Research* with the Association for Institutional Research (AIR), serving as the 2016 President of the California Association of Institutional Research, teaching and developing institutional research and higher education administration courses at four institutions, conducting policy education research at the Florida Legislature, and admissions advisor at the State University of New York, College at Brockport.

Kristina earned her doctorate from Florida State University in Educational Leadership and Policy Studies with a concentration in Higher Education Policy, a Master's in Higher Education Administration from Florida State University, and a Bachelor of Science from the State University of New York, College at Brockport. She publishes and presents in the areas of higher education administration and organization, institutional research, as well as student success with a focus on retention and graduation rates using national databases and institutional data. Her books, *Organization and Administration in Higher Education* (second edition 2017) and *Cultivating a Data*

Culture in Higher Education (2018) are published by Routledge. She has served as issue co-editor and author for *New Directions of Institutional Research*.

CHAPTER AUTHORS

Stephan C. Cooley, MS is Project Analyst for Research and Initiatives with the Association for Institutional Research. He supports AIR's efforts to advance the practice and student success agenda of data professionals in the ever-evolving field of higher education. Stephan serves as the Managing Editor of The AIR Professional File and contributes to the conception and development of the Association's educational opportunities. He previously coordinated AIR's online professional development opportunities for IPEDS Keyholders. Prior to AIR, Stephan served as the lead research assistant for three studies funded by the Institute of Education Sciences examining effective school leadership. He holds an MS in foreign and second language education and BA in French from Florida State University.

Molly K. Ellis, PhD Candidate holds a Master's in Education with a focus in Higher Education from Southern Methodist University and a Bachelor's degree in Economics from Trinity University. Molly's experience includes projects related to pedagogy, course evaluations, community development, organizational leadership, and educational policy initiatives. Her academic research interests include faculty development, organizational leadership, and the policies and infrastructures that surround such in higher education. She has several studies in journal articles and book chapters including in *Journal of the Professoriate* and *Journal of Higher Education*.

Ivan L. Harrell, II, PhD serves as the President of Tacoma Community College (TCC) in Washington state. Having a passion for community college education, Dr. Harrell strives every day to lead a group of professionals in providing the best environment, programs, and services students need to complete their academic and career goals. Prior to TCC, Dr. Harrell most recently served as the Executive Vice President of Academic & Student Affairs at Georgia Piedmont Technical College. Before Georgia Piedmont, he served as the Vice President of Success at Lone Star College, Dean of Student Services at Anne Arundel Community College, Coordinator for Student Affairs at J. Sargeant Reynolds Community College, and Assistant to the Vice President at Tallahassee Community College. Dr. Harrell has written or co-written a number of scholarly articles and book chapters. He has also served as a presenter at numerous local, regional, and national conferences and seminars. He is most proud of his work around improving the success of students of color, particularly Black men, first-generation college students, as well as students who come from traditionally marginalized backgrounds. Dr. Harrell completed his doctor of philosophy degree (PhD) at Florida State University, where he defended his award-winning dissertation, titled, "Using Student Characteristics to Predict the Persistence of Community College Students Enrolled in Online Courses." He holds a master's degree (MEd) from Vanderbilt University, and a bachelor's degree (BA) from Wittenberg University. A native of Oberlin, Ohio, Dr. Harrell was a first-generation student who began his career in community colleges at Tallahassee Community College. Inspired by the diverse, intelligent and hard-working students he met at Tallahassee, Dr. Harrell decided to dedicate his career to advance the community college mission. His goal, as a higher education leader, is to support as many community college students possible to achieve their academic and career goals.

Michael S. Harris, EdD is Associate Professor of higher education and director of the Center for Teaching Excellence at Southern Methodist University in Dallas, Texas. His primary research interests consider the culture, strategy, and behavior of higher education institutions. Harris has taught graduate courses in organization and governance, academic leadership, organizational theory, and the history of American higher education. His work has been published in leading higher education journals such as *The Journal of Higher Education, Research in Higher Education, Innovative Higher Education*, and reported by *The Chronicle of Higher Education* and other media outlets. He is the author of the *The Qualitative Dissertation in Education: A Guide for Integrating Research and Practice* (Routledge, 2019), *How to Get Tenure: Strategies for Successfully Navigating the Process* (Routledge, 2019), *Teaching for Learning: 101 Intentionally-Designed Educational Activities to Put Students on the Path to Success* (Routledge, 2016) with co-authors Claire H. Major and Todd Zakrajsek, and *Understanding Institutional Diversity in American Higher Education* (Jossey-Bass, 2013).

Angela E. Henderson, PhD serves as Director of Institutional Research & Effectiveness at Stetson University, where she is responsible for development and dissemination of institutional data reports and analytics. Henderson's areas of expertise and interest include data-informed analyses, data visualization, and integration of data to guide institutional decision making processes. Throughout her 16 years of higher education experience, she has presented and published on these topics, most recently serving as co-editor of *Cultivating a Data Culture in Higher Education* (2018).

BIOGRAPHIES

Resche D. Hines, PhD is a results-driven, focused, and effectual leader. He has demonstrated throughout his career in Higher Education the proven ability to provide enhanced organizational leadership through data-informed decision making in academic affairs, strategic planning, enrollment management and institutional change management. He has implemented and led efforts to enhance collaborations to strengthen data-informed decision making processes in support of University strategic strategies and initiatives. His educational background and training is in Educational Administration (Ph.D., Michigan State University) and Community Psychology (M.S., Florida A&M University).

Erin J. Holmes, PhD is Associate Vice Provost for Institutional Research at the University of Alaska Anchorage where she leads efforts to create a robust data strategy. She has worked in Institutional Research since 1994. Involved in accreditation, mandatory reporting, and accountability efforts, she is an evaluator corps member for the Northwest Commission on Colleges and Universities. She is educator and assistant instructor with the Association for Institutional Research (AIR) for the Integrated Postsecondary Education Data System (IPEDS) workshops. Research interests include student success and behaviors, policy evaluation, and impacts. Her PhD is in Public Policy and Public Administration from Mississippi State University. Dr. Holmes has published in the *Journal of Public Management & Social Policy* and *Proceedings of the 6th and 7th Annual National Symposium on Student Retention*. She has also contributed book chapters in several books.

Braden J. Hosch, PhD is the Associate Vice President for Institutional Research, Planning, and Effectiveness at Stony Brook University where he leads all aspects of institutional research, helps shape policy and planning, and oversees institutional effectiveness efforts. Braden led adoption of a data governance structure at Stony Brook University and is the principal architect of Stony Brook's data strategy. He has also overseen the integration of institutional research and business intelligence on the campus. In addition, he has published on topics as diverse as the impact of motivation on student learning outcome assessment, benchmarking sources in higher education, and inconsistencies in how institutions determine student living costs. He has served as a national IPEDS trainer for over a decade and regularly conducts national benchmarking studies using a range of national data sets. In prior positions, he has served as the Chief Policy and Research Officer at the Connecticut Board of Regents for Higher Education and the Director of Policy, Finance, and Academic Affairs at the Connecticut Department of Higher Education. Braden is a member of the North East Association for Institutional Research Steering Committee and chairs the Finance Committee, and he was the four-year public university representative to the National Postsecondary Education Cooperative—an advisory body to the U.S. Dept. of Education for higher education data collections. He holds PhD and MA degrees from the University of Wisconsin-Madison, an MA degree from the University of Texas-Dallas, and a B.A. degree from Swarthmore College.

Sheri Jones, MA is Senior Vice President of University Services & Strategic Planning at Ashford University. Ms. Jones's career in higher education spans more than 25 years. Before her promotion to Senior Vice President of University Services and Strategic Planning, she served as Vice President of Administrative Services. In this role, Ms. Jones was responsible for the creation of three essential functional areas related to Ashford's online student modality: the Office of Institutional Research, the Office of Policy and Implementation, and a team specializing in Online Student and Alumni Affairs, including Disability Services and Career Services. She has participated in a number of additional projects which demonstrate her fluency in licensure, accreditation, and legal compliance; information system planning and implementation; and the institutionalization of contemporary University policies and procedures. Ms. Jones is a member of multiple professional associations, including the Society for College and University Planners (SCUP), the Council of College and Military Educators (CCME), and the Association of Governing Boards of Universities and Colleges (AGB). Ms. Jones also serves on the Board of Directors for the San Diego Regional Chamber of Commerce, the San Diego Economic Development Center, and Big Brothers Big Sisters of San Diego. She regularly presents at national conferences and to senior leaders. She holds a M.S. in Education with a Specialization in Leadership for Higher Education from Capella University in Minneapolis, Minnesota, and a B.S. in Psychology from Averett University in Danville, Virginia. Prior to joining the Ashford University team, Ms. Jones served in various leadership positions in higher education, including Director of Student Services and Administration for Argosy University in Sarasota, Florida; and Director of Student Services for the Georgia School of Professional Psychology in Atlanta, Georgia.

Sandra Kinney, MPA is a Senior Director of Institutional Research and Planning at the Georgia Institute of Technology. She has over 25 years of higher education experience in higher education administration with a focus on institutional research, data warehouse design, business intelligence tools, and enterprise resource planning (ERP) implementation. Sandra was heavily involved in the planning and development of Georgia's state longitudinal data system. She has served on the National Postsecondary Education Cooperative (NPEC) and participated in the policy working group in the Post-Collegiate Outcomes collaborative project funded by the Bill & Melinda Gates Foundation. Sandra has been a contributing author on more than 30 national publications for the government and think tank organizations and has given more than 50 presentations on her work.

Shannon Rose LaCount, EdD is Vice President of Campus Strategy at Campus Labs. Dr. LaCount's career in higher education has been shaped by one core belief: an intentional approach to classroom teaching and learning highlights opportunities for growth, for both the student and the teacher. She helps campuses apply and extend this approach to capture all manner of learning, regardless of where it occurs on campus. Her focus is helping institutions transform their data-enabled information into strategic insights that can improve outcomes assessment. Before joining Campus Labs, she served as both an administrator and faculty member at the University of Minnesota Duluth. As Director of Student Learning Assessment, she led a campus-wide assessment process for academic departments and student life programs and served as the Accreditation Liaison to the Higher Learning Commission. Dr. LaCount often presents at national assessment and accreditation conferences. She publishes regularly on www.campusintelligence.com, and was a contributing author to Engagement and Employability: Integrating Career Learning Through Co-curricular Experiences in Postsecondary Education.

Erez Lenchner, PhD serves as the Associate Provost for Institutional Effectiveness at CUNY John Jay College. His research focuses on optimization problems and educational data mining in higher education, in support of student-level real-time behaviors analysis, and student success initiatives. Throughout his research portfolio, Dr. Lenchner links multiple dynamic and static information systems to support data-driven decision making. His research and teaching in IR crosses two and four-year institutions as well as system, state, and national IR systems. He serves as a national Integrated Postsecondary Education Data System (IPEDS) Educator for the National Center for Education Statistics (NCES)/Association for Institutional Research (AIR). Previously, he served as a visiting Associate Professor of Institutional Research and Higher Education at Hokkaido University, and as the Senior Institutional Researcher at LaGuardia Community College. Dr. Lenchner has made over 50 national and international presentations as well as regularly published in peer-review publications in higher education and biomedical journals.

Jason R. Lewis, CPA is Deputy Director and Chief Financial Officer of the Association for Institutional Research. He leads the AIR education team to develop new education products and opportunities, and to design models for reframing the work of IR and related fields. In addition, as CFO, his duties include oversight for the organization's financial and accounting operations, as well as all banking, investment, insurance, audit, and tax compliance matters related to the Association. Jason holds a CPA and a BA in Accounting from University of Florida.

Derek MacPherson, MA is a Senior IT Analyst at Zovio and has been an information systems and data analysis for more than 20 years in a variety of industries, including higher education, telecom, and architecture. He has a Bachelor of Arts in History/Political Science and a minor in Computer Programing from Point Loma Nazarene University, a Master of Arts in History from San Diego State University, and a Master of Arts in Defense and Strategic Studies from the Naval War College. He has mostly recently co-authored, with Kristina Powers, "Leading Gainful Employment Metric Reporting" in *New Directions for Institutional Research: Postgraduate Outcomes of College Students*.

Kim Nelson Pryor, MA is a doctoral student in the Annette Simmons School of Education at Southern Methodist University. She holds a BA in English and Classical and Medieval Studies from Bates College, an MA in the Humanities from the University of Chicago, and an MEd in Curriculum and Instruction from The University of Texas at Austin. Prior to pursuing her doctorate, she worked as a high school English teacher and adult educator, a student affairs professional, and a community college instructor. Her research synthesizes her experiences at many levels of education to explore how secondary and postsecondary curriculum can best foster students' identity development and self-advocacy, as well as promote equitable academic and personal outcomes for all students.

Leah Ewing Ross, PhD is Senior Director for Research and Initiatives with the Association for Institutional Research. She leads AIR's national research, scholarship, and innovation agenda to effectively position IR within the changing landscape of higher education. Leah partners with stakeholders to create forward-looking models to advance evidenced-based decision making, and to equip higher education professionals with the knowledge and tools they need as leaders within their organizations. Leah's recent publications include *Data-Informed Decision Cultures* (Ross & Lewis, 2017, AIR); *A New Vision for Institutional Research* (Swing & Ross, 2016, Change* magazine); *Statement of Aspirational Practice for Institutional Research* (Swing & Ross, 2016, AIR); and *Student Affairs Assessment in the Broader Institutional Context: Values, Ethics, and Politics* (Kennedy-Phillips & Ross, 2019). Prior to AIR, Leah worked in consulting, scholarly publications, association management, and college admissions. She holds a PhD in Educational Leadership from Iowa State University, MS in Higher Education Administration from Florida State University, and an AB in English from Mount Holyoke College.

Jason Lee Wang, PhD is a Senior Decision Support Analyst in the Office of Institutional Research and Planning at Georgia Institute of Technology. He received his PhD in Bioengineering and MS and BS in Mechanical Engineering and has co-authored several peer-reviewed publications and conference presentations. Jason's work focuses on data analysis, developing data visualizations, data strategy for institutional research, and combining federal and institutional data to inform higher education decision making. He has contributed to multiple projects developing data strategy within changing IT infrastructures. Reflecting his interests in engineering education and international experiences, Jason has taught engineering mechanics courses at Georgia Tech's Atlanta campus and Oxford study abroad program.

Steven A. Weiner, MBA is President of Menlo College. Steven completed his graduate studies at the University of Chicago. He then worked at the university for 16 years, the last eight of which were in the role of Associate Dean and Principal Business Officer at the Pritzker School of Medicine. After Chicago, he spent 10 years in the consulting world, first as Vice President & Division Manager for Science Applications International, and then as Vice President for First Consulting Group. He left First Consulting to co-found an open source medical software start-up company, which he sold just prior to his return to higher education at Menlo College in 2013. When he's not in his home on the Menlo College campus in Atherton, he can be found tending a small vineyard and way too many olive trees on property he owns in Sonoma County.

Michael J. Weisman, MBA is Vice President of Campus Relations at Campus Labs. In 2001, Michael Weisman co-founded Campus Labs while pursuing his MBA at the University at Buffalo. What started out as a simple way to collect student feedback is today an enterprise software platform offering a complete set of data-driven solutions to more than 1,300 colleges and universities. Mr. Weisman feeds his curiosity about higher education and his passion for impeccable client service by visiting campuses, speaking with administrators, faculty, and staff to learn about their unique challenges and addressing solutions offered by Campus Labs. He remains committed to helping colleges and universities find the solutions that can best serve students. Mr. Weisman regularly participates and presents at higher education conferences including Association for

Institutional Research (AIR), Educause, Middle States Council on Higher Education (MSCHE), National Association of Student Personnel Administrators (NASPA), Northeastern Association of Schools and Colleges (NEASC), Society of College and University Planners (SCUP), and the WASC Senior Commission on Universities and Colleges (WSCUC).

Index

Abai, M. 6, 7, 11
academic analytics 128, 134, 156–157
academic performance data 120, 157
access 14, 17, 25–27, 29; data governance 106; data hoarders 109; institutional research 157, 161, 164–165; IT planning 58, 60, 66, 67; presidents and provosts 121, 122, 125; self-appraisal 88, 94; training for data consumers 164, 165; unauthorized 62
accessibility 25–26, 100, 122, 125, 164
accountability 10, 46, 98, 117, 118; faculty 135; high stakes 139; metrics 136; presidents and provosts 119; stakeholder engagement 111; updates 51
accreditation documents 76, 101–102, 108
accreditation process 135
accuracy of data 12, 24, 50, 124, 163
action-focused agenda 153
action steps 45–46, 47, 65
actionable data 56, 72, 138, 139, 159, 168, 176
adaptability 48, 55–56
Adelman, S. 6, 7, 11
administrators 100
advantage 50; *see also* competitive advantage
affinity mapping 48–49

aggregated data 169–170, 171, 175, 176
Allison, M. 39
Amazon Web Services 32
analytical ability 175–176
analytics 14, 17, 21, 28, 54, 59; academic 128, 134, 156–157; descriptive 30–31; IT planning 58, 66; learning 100; predictive 30–31, 181; student affairs 148; text 105; tools 32
application programming interface (API) 19, 20
archives 162
artificial intelligence 30, 181
assessment: continuous improvement 58; formative and summative 133; program 76; self-appraisal 86, 87; strategic planning 37–38, 46; student affairs 149–150
assessment management systems (AMSs) 100
Association for Institutional Research (AIR) 147
audiences 99–102, 146–147
audits, software 109

Baier, L. 32
Baker, R. S. 157
Banner 14, 17
Batini, C. 24, 25
benchmarks 100, 128, 136, 147

193

INDEX

BI tool 32–33, 174
big data 4, 64, 111, 164
British Library 15
budgets 10, 37–38, 51, 146
business analysts 172
business intelligence 5, 32, 66, 175
business transactions 59
buy-in 33, 86, 87, 135–136, 149–150, 180

Campus Labs 112
campus-specific applications 173
capture 18–19
Carruthers, C. 16
centers of excellence (COEs) 178
centralization 41, 103, 108, 178
change: adaptability to 48, 55–56; change management 110–112; resistance to 37, 43
change management specialists 172
chief planning officers (CPOs) 40, 41, 47
Classification of Instructional Programs (CIP) 105
data cleaning 23–24, 25
Cleveland, H. 72
cloud services 110
coding of data 105
cognitive biases 180–181
Cognos 32
collaboration 86, 95
college strategic plans 75
committees 21, 47
communication: campus culture 139; IT analysts 182; self-appraisal 88, 90; stakeholder engagement 111; strategic planning 40, 43–44, 47
comparative data 17
competitive advantage 33, 38, 50, 66, 72
compliance 66, 67, 172
confidentiality 80
confirmation bias 177–178, 180–181
Conlin, M. 6

continuous improvement 55, 56, 58–59, 112, 135; IT planning 60, 66; presidents and provosts 126; self-appraisal 91; student affairs 150
Contreras-McGavin, M. 136
Cooley, Stephan C. 84–97
costs: accessibility 26; analytics 31; integrated data strategy and IT planning 66; student affairs 146, 147
CRM *see* customer relationship management
Crystal Reports 32, 174
culture of data use 88, 91, 112; *see also* data culture
culture of evidence 147, 150
culture of inquiry 88, 92
curation 21
curriculum design 98
curriculum planning 158
customer relationship management (CRM) 103, 108, 169, 175
cyberattacks 62–63

Dalkir, K. 74
DalleMule, L. 72
data 3–4; definitions 135, 179–180; DIKW model 73–74; faculty 128–129, 132–137; identification 15, 16–18, 54, 57; IT analysts 169–170, 175–177, 178–181; leveraging existing 73, 74–81, 102; reusability 15, 16, 19, 55, 66; strategic planning 37, 38, 39; *see also* information
data access 14, 17, 25–27; data governance 106; data hoarders 109; institutional research 157, 161, 164–165; IT planning 58, 60, 66, 67; presidents and provosts 121, 122, 125; self-appraisal 88, 94; training for data consumers 164, 165; unauthorized 62
data acquisition 14, 16–21, 54, 57, 66

INDEX

data analysis 4, 66; data warehouses 169; IT analysts 170; multiple approaches to 5; redundant 49; research design 81; student affairs 147, 148; tools 32; training for data consumers 164
DATA analysis 50–51
data analytics *see* analytics
data capital 33
data capture 18–19
data collection: challenges 102–104; data governance 106; faculty 100, 137; IT analysts 169; IT planning 57; multiple approaches to 5; new technologies 53; redundant 49; research methods 78–79; scheduling 126; secondary 77–78; self-appraisal 88, 90; strategic planning 37; student affairs 101, 148, 149–150; trends in 126; useful data 6–7
data culture 44–45, 55, 121–122, 176, 179, 180, 182; *see also* culture of data use
data/disaster recovery plans (DRPs) 162
data-discovery tools 71–72
data extraction 14, 17, 29, 58, 66
data fatigue 137–138
data fluency 111–112
data function 86, 87, 91
data governance 14, 15–16, 17, 21–23, 54–55, 59; Campus Labs 112; confidence in data 12; data governance analysts 172; data security 62, 64; definition of terms 180; institutional research 162; IT planning 58, 60, 66–67; policies 177; sharing data 106
data hoarders 99, 108–109
data integrity 8, 160, 163
data lakes 19, 20, 32
data literacy 7, 14, 17, 28, 54; change management 111; IT planning 58, 66; self-appraisal 88, 93
data management 175
data marts 175

data mining 72–73, 156–157, 158, 159
data ownership 160, 161
data preparation 4, 9
data processing 15, 54, 58
data production: multiple approaches to 5; self-appraisal 85, 86, 88, 94
data professionals 87, 101–102, 124–125; *see also* information technology analysts
data quality 14, 16, 17, 23–25, 28; confidence in 12; institutional research 159; IT planning 66, 67; self-appraisal 88, 93; student affairs 150–151
data sources 12, 99, 102–104, 107, 161, 177
data stewards 22–23, 25, 28
data strategy: affinity mapping 49; backward design 98; benefits of a good 5–6; challenges and solutions 98, 99–110; characteristics 55–57; core elements 54–55; definition of 4–5, 72; faculty perspective 137–139; inclusive 112–113; institutional research 72, 159–161, 164–165; investment in 3; IT analysts 168, 170–173; IT planning 53, 57–59, 61, 65–67; key elements 14–36; leadership commitment 8–12; one-plan approach 65; presidents and provosts 118–119; purpose of 55, 99; self-appraisal 84–97; strategic planning 39, 41–48; student affairs 148; two-plan approach 65–66; updates 51; value of creating a 5; *see also* strategy
data structure 99, 105
data tools *see* tools
data triangulation 81
data usage 14, 17, 28, 54; faculty 139; IT planning 58, 66; presidents and provosts 121; reporting 30; self-appraisal 88, 91
data warehouses 18, 19, 179, 180; data extraction 29; definition of 175; IT analysts 169, 172; tools 32

195

INDEX

database administrators (DBAs) 171, 172
databases 107, 108–109, 158, 173–174, 175
Davenport, T. 9, 72
deadlines 152
decentralization 41–42, 178–179
decision making 4, 5–6, 55; data governance 21; data vision 15; data warehouses 169; faculty 128; IT analysts 170; IT planning 66; presidents and provosts 117; self-appraisal 88, 90, 94; strategic planning 37, 42–43, 44; student affairs 143, 147–148
demands 49, 50, 65, 139, 179
democratization of data 28, 65, 71–72
demographic changes 145
demographic data 105, 106, 119–120
department plans 73, 75
departments 7, 44
descriptive analytics 30–31
detail data 169, 171, 175
dictionaries 22, 23, 24, 25
DIKW (Data-Information-Knowledge-Wisdom) model 73–74
discipline 9
dissemination 54, 99–100
distributed data model 7
diversity 119
document imaging repositories 18
duplication 44, 50–51, 66, 101, 178–179
Dykes, B. 29

Eaton, J. S. 135
educational data mining (EDM) 156–157
EDUCAUSE 110, 147
Ehlert, Jason 110
enrollments 75, 103, 105, 108; confidentiality 80; institutional research 155–156; presidents and provosts 120; requests for data 101–102

enterprise resource planning (ERP) 18, 103, 108, 169
environment 40, 44–45, 47
equity 118, 119
error reporting 25, 163
ethical issues 79–80, 164
ETL *see* extract-transform-load
European Union 27, 64
evaluation: continuous improvement 58; end-of-course 133; self-appraisal 85; strategic planning 37–38
evidence-based culture 147, 150
Excel 174
executive summaries 107, 123, 124, 169
existing information 73, 74–81, 102
extract-transform-load (ETL) 20, 22, 32, 169, 172, 175

facilities access data 18
faculty 128–141; activity data 17; analytics 31; as an audience 100–101; challenges with data 134–137; departmental plans 75; difficulties faced by 131–132; hiring 120, 134; improving data strategy 137–139; IT analysts' reports 170–171; lack of training 125; roles and responsibilities 129–131; senate structure 41; student-level data 133–134
Fair and Accurate Credit Transactions Act (FACTA) 63
Family Education Rights and Privacy Act (FERPA) 26, 63, 110, 161–162
Federal Information Security Management Act (FISMA) 63
feedback 92, 182
file shares 19, 20
finances 121, 146
flexibility 56
Floyd, N. 75
formative assessment 133

INDEX

Free Application for Federal Student Aid (FAFSA) 19, 27
Fuller, M. B. 150

Gagliardi, J. S. 122
Gartner 33
gatekeepers 103
General Data Protection Regulation (GDPR) 27, 64
goals 5, 14–15, 56; alignment with 55; analytics 58; data governance 21; decentralized leadership 42; identification of 59; IT planning 54, 57, 65, 66; need for defined 84–85; prioritization 18; self-appraisal 88, 89, 95; software 109; strategic planning 37–38, 39–40, 43, 44, 45–46, 47; strategy updates 51; *see also* objectives
Google Cloud Platform 32
governance 14, 15–16, 17, 21–23, 54–55, 59; Campus Labs 112; confidence in data 12; data governance analysts 172; data security 62, 64; definition of terms 180; institutional research 162; IT planning 58, 60, 66; policies 177; sharing data 106
Gower, M. 74
grades 100
graduation rates 105, 108, 120
Gramm-Leach-Bliley Act (GLBA) 26–27, 63

hardware 61, 64, 65
Harrell, II, Ivan L. 117–127
Harris, Michael S. 128–141
Harris, Molly K. 128–141
Health Insurance Portability and Accountability Act (HIPAA) 22, 26, 63, 110
Heaton, J. 77
Henderson, Angela E. 37–52
Higher Education Cloud Vendor Assessment Tool (HECVAT) 110

Hines, Resche D. 37–52
Hinton, K. E. 42
Holmes, Erin J. 71–83
Hosch, Braden J. 14–36
Hughes, S. L. 122
IBM Cloud 32

identification 15, 16–18, 54, 57
inclusion 119
information: DIKW model 73–74; existing 74–81; existing information 102; presidents and provosts 123–124; retention of 161; trust in 152; useful types of 78; *see also* data
information technology (IT) 16, 53–68, 112; commonalities of data strategy and IT plan 57–59; core elements of a data strategy 54–55; core elements of an IT plan 59–60; data security 61–64; data stewards 22; data strategy characteristics 55–57; feedback requests 137; one-plan approach 64–65; purpose of data strategy 55; two-plan approach 65–66; *see also* software; tools
information technology (IT) analysts 168–183; challenges 178–181; clear data requests 181–182; context and detail 182; description of 169–170; difficult components of the position 173–178; existing activities 170–173; new data systems 182; positions 171–173
infrastructure 33, 51; data 112, 121, 126; IT 54–55, 59, 61, 64, 65, 66
initiative fatigue 150
innovation 55, 58, 66, 86, 113
inquiry, culture of 88, 92
institutional research (IR) 122, 151, 155–167; challenges 159–164; data function 86; data professionals 101; difficult components of IR positions 156–157; IT analysts 171; leveraging

197

INDEX

existing information 74–81; models of 71–73; roles 155–156
Institutional Review Boards (IRBs) 79–80, 130, 164
Integrated Postsecondary Education Data Systems (IPEDS) 17, 19, 29, 101
integration 14–15, 16, 54; challenges 180; data strategy and IT planning 58, 65; tools 32
inventories 16–18, 30, 74
investment 3, 5–6, 8–9, 51
IPEDS *see* Integrated Postsecondary Education Data Systems
IR *see* institutional research
iterative approach 182

Jackson, P. 16
Jones, Sheri 142–154
journals 130, 134

Kaye, J. 39
key indicators 87, 88, 90–95
key performance indicators (KPIs) 58, 59, 66
key questions 87–90
Kezar, A. 136
Kinney, Sandra 53–68
Kirby, Y. K. 75
Kiron, D. 16, 28
Knauf, R. 157–158
knowledge 72–74, 142
knowledge management 155, 157, 160, 162–163

LaCount, Shannon Rose 98–114
Lahanas, S. 4–5, 72
Lane, F. C. 150
leadership 7, 8–12, 107–108; aggregated data 169; engagement 111–112; presidents and provosts 117–127; strategic planning 40–42, 47; student affairs 145–148; transformational 99, 112

learning management systems (LMSs) 17, 18, 19, 29, 100, 169, 173, 175
learning outcomes 37–38, 101–102, 135, 158, 170
legacy technology 65, 66, 155
legislation 26–27, 63, 110
Lenchner, Erez 155–167
Levy, E. 15
Lewis, Jason R. 84–97
library data 17
linkage 19–21
LMSs *see* learning management systems

Maas, B. 74
machine learning 30, 53, 181
MacPherson, Derek 168–183
Marr, B. 5–6, 11
Martin, Roger 72
master data management (MDM) 23
McTighe, J. 98
metadata 22
methods-focused agenda 153
metrics 28, 30, 58, 59; faculty 134; IT analysts 170; IT planning 66; quantitative data 136
Microsoft Excel 174
Microsoft SQL Server 32, 174
missing data 24
mission 15, 18, 54–55; goals 45, 46; strategic planning 37–38, 40, 42–43, 47
Moss, L. 6, 7, 11
multiple data sources 103–104, 177

naming conventions 105, 106, 107
National Association of Student Personnel Administrators (NASPA) 143–144, 147
National Center for Education Statistics (NCES) 105
National Student Clearinghouse (NSC) 16
National Survey of Student Engagement (NSSE) 78, 79, 80

network usage data 18
Nickerson, R. S. 177–178, 180
Nissenbaum, H. 162
non-tenure-track faculty (NTTF) 129–130, 131, 132

objectives 47, 56; identification of 59; IT planning 57, 65; prioritization 18; strategic planning 37–38, 45–46; *see also* goals
Offerman, L. 42
Open Database Connectivity (ODBC) 19–20
ops engineers 172
Oracle 32, 174
organizational change 37, 43
organizational culture 44, 51
Otto, B. 21

packaging information 124
participants 88, 90
partners 74–75
PeopleSoft 14, 17
performance assessment 45–46
performance measures 134
permissions 101, 106, 109, 161
persistence 9, 10
personally identifiable information (PII) 62–63, 64, 110
personnel 98, 99, 107–108
perspective 88, 89
plans 10–11, 38, 39, 53–68, 77; *see also* strategic planning
Plotkin, D. 22
policies 66, 109; data access 161; IT analysts 173–174, 177; security 27; self-appraisal 88, 95
Post-it notes 48
Powers, Kristina 3–13
predictive analytics 30–31, 181
Prentice, P. 28
presidents 117–127, 170

prioritization 15, 18, 20; IT planning 58; strategic planning 37–38, 51
privacy 25, 27, 28, 63; data security 62; faculty concerns 138; institutional research 80, 161–162, 164; IT planning 60
product managers 172
productivity measures 128
professional development 88, 93, 100–101, 103, 110; *see also* training
program reviews 76, 101–102
project managers 171–172
project planning 59, 60
provosts 117–127
Pryor, Kim Nelson 128–141

qualitative data 77, 79, 126, 137
quality assurance (QA) 172, 173, 175
quality of data 14, 16, 17, 23–25, 28; confidence in 12; institutional research 159; IT planning 66, 67; self-appraisal 88, 93; student affairs 150–151
quantitative data 77, 105, 136–137
quantity of data 151

Ransbotham, S. 28
Rao, V. R. 73
redundancies 49, 55, 86
relational databases 173–174, 175
report inventories 74
reporting 6, 14, 17, 21, 29–30, 59; aggregated data 169; data professionals 101–102; definitions 179–180; demand for data 179; faculty buy-in 135–136; goals 46; institutional research 155–156, 160, 162, 164; IT analysts 170–171, 182; IT planning 58, 66; signing off 10, 12; student affairs 148; tools 32
requests for data 101–102, 137–138, 151, 177–179, 180–182
research data stores 14–15

INDEX

research design 81
research faculty 130–131, 134
research methodology 76–81
residence hall management systems 18
resources 15, 33, 51; equitable outcomes 118; IT planning 59, 60, 61, 65, 66; strategic planning 38, 40–41; student affairs 146, 147
retention of information 161
reusability 15, 16, 19, 55, 66
revenue 31
risk: analytics 31; data security 62, 110; risk assessment 64
roadmaps 59, 60, 66, 95
Romero, C. 157
Ross, Leah Ewing 71, 73, 84–97
rubrics 100

Sakurai, Y. 157–158
secondary data collection 77–78
security 16, 25–27, 28, 99, 110; institutional research 161–162; IT planning 61–64, 66, 67
self-appraisal 84–97; key indicators 87, 88, 90–95; key questions 87–90
self-serving bias 180
Serban, A. M. 155
service delivery: IT planning 59, 60; student affairs 145–146, 147
service role of faculty 131
sharing data 99, 103, 106–107, 110–111, 138, 143
signing off 10, 12
Silicon Valley Data Science group 64
SISs *see* student information systems
Soares, L. 122
social media 18
software 99, 109–110; data infrastructure 121; faculty learning 136; feedback on 137; IT analysts 173; IT planning 60, 61, 64, 65; security 110; *see also* tools

software as service (SAS) model 109
SQL (Sequential Query Language) 173, 174
stakeholders 86–87, 118–119; data collection 103; data governance 66; data strategy creation 108; definition of terms 180; engagement 111; inclusion of 56, 59; institutional research 156; involvement in design 112; IT analysts 170; listening to 113; resistance to change 43; self-appraisal 90, 91; strategic planning 38, 40, 43–44, 47; student affairs 146–147, 150
Stanford University 27
statistical tools 32
Statistics Canada 24
stewards 22–23, 25, 28
stewardship 21, 112; IT planning 66; Stanford University 27; strategic planning 38
Stony Brook University 16, 23, 28
storage 15, 19; institutional research 161, 162; IT planning 57; new technologies 53; tools 32
strategic planning 10–11, 37–52; affinity mapping 48–49; college or departmental plans 75; communication 43–44, 47; DATA analysis 50–51; data strategy contrasted with 46–48; environmental scan 44–45, 47; goals, objectives, and action steps 45–46, 47; leadership 40–42, 47; mission, vision, and values 42–43, 47; student affairs 148, 149; SWOT analysis 49–50; updates 51
strategy: definition of 38, 72; planning distinction 39; updates 51; *see also* data strategy
Strong, D. M. 159
structured data 105
student affairs 101, 142–154; data challenges 148–151; demographic

changes 145; IT analysts' reports 171; positions 143–144; reliance on data 147–148; stakeholder priorities 146–147; timeliness of response 145–146
student information systems (SISs) 14–15, 103, 169, 175; centralization 108; IT analysts 173; security issues 62–63; sharing data 106–107
student-level data 133–134, 170–171, 182
students: as an audience 102; engagement 78–79, 80; self-appraisal 88, 91–92; student success 31, 85, 87, 101, 147, 162; student voice 126; support for 102, 119, 142, 144
summative assessment 133
support for students 102, 119, 142, 144
surveys 6–7, 18, 78–79; collection methods 104; follow-up 28; reporting 30; student affairs 143–144
sustainability 56
Swing, R. 71, 72, 73
SWOT analysis 49–50
systems thinking 106

Tableau 32, 174
Takada, K. 157–158
teaching 130
technology 53–68, 108, 111–112; changes in 155, 161; faculty learning 136; incorporation of new technologies 181; *see also* information technology; software
tenure-track faculty 129–130, 131, 132, 139
terminology 174, 175, 179–180
text analytics 105
time frames 45, 47, 48, 61, 152
time management 131–132, 149

timeliness: DATA analysis 50; data quality 24; IT analysts 168; student affairs services 145–146
tools 31–33, 99, 109–110; data-discovery 71–72; data-mining 72–73; IT analysts 174; *see also* software
training 103, 107, 155; data consumers 159, 160, 163–164, 165; data security 110; institutional research 159; lack of 122, 125; student affairs 150; technology 108; *see also* professional development
transparency 44, 89, 118, 138
triangulation of data 81
Tromp, S. 44
Tsuruta, S. 157–158

University of Michigan 27
University of Washington 28
unstructured data 105
usage 14, 17, 28, 54; faculty 139; IT planning 58, 66; presidents and provosts 121; reporting 30; self-appraisal 88, 91

validation 24–25
value-added data strategy 56
values 38, 42–43, 46, 47, 61
Vartanian, T. P. 77–78
vendor-based systems 17
Ventura, S. 157
verification 163
vision 4–5, 15, 61; campus culture 139; goals 45; integrated data strategy and IT planning 66; self-appraisal 88, 89; stakeholder engagement 111; strategic planning 38, 40, 42–43, 47
Volkwein, J. F. 71

Wang, Jason Lee 53–68
Wang, R. Y. 159
Webber, K. L. 156
websites 133–134

201

INDEX

Weiner, Steven 3–13
Weisman, Michael J. 98–114
Wiggins, G. 98
Wilkinson, P. J. 122

Williams, L. 159
wisdom 72, 73–74

Yacef, K. 157

Printed in the United States
by Baker & Taylor Publisher Services